*Family Assessment Handbook*

# Family Assessment Handbook

AN INTRODUCTORY PRACTICE GUIDE TO FAMILY ASSESSMENT
AND INTERVENTION

## Barbara Thomlison
FLORIDA INTERNATIONAL UNIVERSITY

BROOKS/COLE

THOMSON LEARNING

Australia • Canada • Mexico • Singapore • Spain • United Kingdom • United States

**BROOKS/COLE**

**THOMSON LEARNING**

Publisher: *Edith Beard Brady*
Executive Acquisitions Editor: *Lisa Gebo*
Assistant Editor: *Shelley Gesicki*
Marketing Team: *Caroline Concilla, Megan Hansen, Tami Strang*
Editorial Assistant: *Sheila Walsh*
Project Editor: *Laurel Jackson*
Production Service: *The Cowans*

Manuscript Editor: *Patterson Lamb*
Permissions Editor: *Sue Ewing*
Cover Design: *Jeanne Calabrese*
Cover Photos: *PhotoDisc*
Interior Illustration: *The Cowans*
Print Buyer: *Vena Dyer*
Typesetting: *The Cowans*
Printing and Binding: *Webcom, Ltd.*

*For more information about this or any other Brooks/Cole product, contact:*
BROOKS/COLE
511 Forest Lodge Road
Pacific Grove, CA 93950 USA
www.brookscole.com
1-800-423-0563 (Thomson Learning Academic Resource Center)

Printed in Canada
10 9 8 7 6 5 4 3

**Library of Congress Cataloging-in-Publication Data**

Thomlison, Barbara
    Family assessment handbook : an introductory practice guide to family assessment and intervention / Barbara Thomlison.
        p. cm.
    Includes bibliographical references and index.
    ISBN 0-534-36598-1
        1. Family social work. 2. Family assessment. I. Title.

HV697.T53 2002
362.82--dc21

2001037772

*To Breanne and Lynn, who believe that the secret to coping is always to look on the positive and humorous side of life events. Thank you for always being positive and inspiring me to keep trying to achieve my very best. I am grateful for all you have taught me. I love you and dedicate this book to you.*

▼▼▼

# *Contents*

D0073780

## *Part One: Family Assessment*  *1*

CHAPTER ONE

## *The Context of Helping Families*  *3*

# Part Three: Practicing Family Assessment: Case Studies 113

# *Preface*

Most human service professionals engage in family assessment activities in their daily practice, and beginning practitioners consider family assessment to be one of the most challenging aspects of their work. Conducting an assessment of family needs and issues is important to understanding how to enhance the social and interpersonal environments of family systems, as well as to determine the extent to which the family may be counted on as a resource. The most common form of family treatment offered by human service organizations is a practical, short-term, family-centered intervention to strengthen family functioning.

There are many family models of practice. As a promising, evidence-based approach to family problems, this book is focused on a multisystemic view of assessment and intervention emphasizing the interrelationships among individual, family, and social support factors. Family-centered interventions are associated with improvements in child developmental status, parenting skill, and family relationships. Recognizing that skills for working with families are not developed solely from reading, practitioners are encouraged to evaluate the family systems of which they are a part and to practice the concepts by case study and discussion using the five cases provided. In addition, practitioners must seek supervision and consultation when working with families in the field, where the real skill is developed, and feedback is important. The book's intent is to offer a beginning perspective to practitioners who must develop a practical understanding of families and the multiple systems with which they interact.

## What the Book Offers

The *Family Assessment Handbook* is a primer in family assessment and intervention planning for social work and human service students and for beginning professionals. The content imparts basic information focused on person-environment or family systems theory, selected empirically supported treatments, and those interventions found to be most useful across different cultural milieus. The goal of the book is to provide introductory information and to describe skills for assessing family functioning, as well as presenting guidelines for clinical assessment and treatment planning. The guidelines are just that; practitioners will not use exactly the same treatment in every case. Practice guidelines offer information for use in the decision-making stages of treatment for the most common family problems.

Family functioning and the problems and needs of the family as whole are described at an introductory level. In addition, assessment is viewed from a developmentally informed perspective with the practitioner seen as part of the interplay of systems interacting with the family. The five case studies that are included focus on particular populations and issues of family functioning. The family journal helps students learn more about their own values, morals, beliefs, and personal family system functioning. All the cases, activities, and concepts emphasize the complex interplay of multisystems. The clinical issues and conceptual approach are directed toward professionals who work in a time-limited setting yet need an effective approach to changing social environments with ethnically and culturally diverse families. The *Family Assessment Handbook* aims to provide practical suggestions for both assessment and intervention activities within a multisystems framework.

## Format of the Book

The book is conceptualized as three interrelated teaching and learning units. Each part emphasizes *application* of concepts for reinforcement of learning. At the end of each chapter are activities to enhance the theory and concepts. Learning activities can be used as separate teaching assignments, either in small groups or through self-directed approaches, and can be applied to the student's family journal or one of the five cases. The book has three parts:

- *Part One* includes six chapters addressing the theory, concepts, and context of family assessment intervention planning.

- *Part Two* is focused on self-assessment and critical thinking using a family journal for illustrating the impact of various systems on individual behavior. Each student can explore his or her family system through the family journal, learning through self-reflection how family environments influence the individual. Critically reflecting on their own family history and beliefs helps students understand how these factors influence their perceptions, attitudes, and responses to those families and individuals seeking service from them. By examining their own family membership and patterns of interaction, students may understand the uniqueness and diversity of the families to whom they apply selected family systems thinking, theory, and concepts. In this way, students learn the systemic approach and the myriad of issues for assessment and planning when doing family practice.

- *Part Three* includes five case studies that illustrate the interplay of family systems, needs, and diversity that occurs among families and their situations. Family case studies are designed to take students through the process of assessment and intervention planning.

The case studies are derived from the author's practice experiences. Case studies are used to

1. Assess unique family issues and concerns
2. Practice family interviewing skills through group role simulations
3. Assess family systems for strengths and resources in planning for interventions
4. Reinforce theory and concepts of multisystemic family assessment
5. Practice organizing information by writing a professional family assessment report
6. Increase students' awareness of their strengths and skills for helping

Finally, the book is written in an informal manner to complement the variety of teaching and preferred learning approaches of instructors and students. Case activities can be used for self-directed learning or group study. Through reading, discovery, and active learning, students gain confidence in developing family assessment and intervention plans. To use the activities and family journal effectively, students need to be in a climate of trust and know that there is no right answer or easily predictable solution. Differences among families are seen as a strength and an opportunity to promote resilience.

## Acknowledgments

I would like to thank the following reviewers for their insightful comments and suggestions: Debra Ingle, Kellogg Community College; Patrick Romine, University of Phoenix; Katherine Shank, Miami University; and José Torres, University of Wisconsin–Milwaukee.

I am indebted to a number of colleagues, friends, and others who contributed to this book in many ways and who tolerated and understood with humor and grace the various drafts of this manuscript. The dedicated staff at Brooks/Cole do not go unnoticed: Thank you, Lisa Gebo, Susan Wilson (and Hannah), Shelley Gesicki, JoAnne von Zastrow, and the rest of the book team for assisting me during the many office moves I experienced. You are a constant source of inspiration and a great team to work with. I would also like to express appreciation and thanks to Cathryn Bradshaw, MSW, for her invaluable research assistance and to the Killam Trust Foundation of the University of Calgary for awarding me a Killam Resident Fellowship for this manuscript. Finally, I am deeply appreciative of the assistance offered by the late Dr. Walter Hudson, social worker, professor, friend, humorist, and wise person, who mentored and coached me in the methodological challenges in validating structured family assessments. Thank you.

## Final Thoughts

It is my hope that each family practice will bring you the same satisfaction that I have experienced over the years. Skill development results from actual work with families across settings. Each new encounter is a learning experience, so each encounter with a family should introduce new understanding of the family as a unique system. Therefore, quality supervision is essential to learning. Working with families is about assisting the individual members to enhance their social and environmental relationships and to find ways to enhance their interactions and connections with one another. Regardless of the issues and concerns, families are the heart of the matter, and family practitioners are strategically positioned to help them by using brief, time-limited, and effective family interventions in practice.

*Barbara Thomlison*

# PART ONE

# Family Assessment

# The Context of Helping Families

Assessing, planning, implementing, and evaluating families and their situations can be daunting for the beginning practitioner. However, you can increase your confidence and competence in handling these tasks if you follow a systematic, best-practice approach to selecting intervention strategies. Before you can plan an intervention to address family issues, you must understand the context in which you help families, as well as the context of the family issues—that is, of the family as a system. Once you know the circumstances that influence the helping process for families, you should be able to provide more effective interventions.

Practitioners must view a family as a system experiencing various types of issues and problems within itself and with the systems with which it interacts. A family systems approach is less individually oriented than other approaches, because it treats the family as a unit. Even so, the individual family members and their actions must considered, and the impact of various systems—especially the family system—on individual behavior is of primary importance. As the family environment is one of the important influences on the individual family members, family experiences play a crucial role in causing, promoting, or reinforcing troubling behaviors of children, adolescents, and adults. Therefore, it is important to develop interventions targeted to parents, siblings, and/or the entire family unit. However, families are not the only influence that shape family members' beliefs and behavior. Others, such as teachers, coaches, child-care providers, neighbors, and community members often influence how a family member feels and behaves. Family interventions to prevent, reduce, or remediate problems frequently need to be complemented by interventions carried out in other systems or settings that impact family members, such as a child-care setting, a school, or another community service system.

Interventions designed to change the values, attitudes, or the behaviors of family units are often challenging and in some situations are costly. A single intervention conducted in isolation is not likely to solve some problems of families, and the most effective approaches include several types of interventions and strategies that complement one another. Realize, too, that even these may fail to reach some families and individuals most in need of change. Carefully consider your skill level, expertise, resources, and community support when selecting interventions. Above all, make sure the interventions you select fit together for addressing the family troubles. Keep in mind that you may need to modify an intervention to make it appropriate to the circumstances, culture, and community. The context of assessing and planning for family interventions is critical.

## Family Defined

As diverse structures and definitions of "family" evolve from gender role shifts and changing attitudes in society, there are debates about what constitutes a family and how family intervention, family practice, and family therapy are defined. Some family model definitions rigidly adhere to treating the entire family unit; other approaches are more flexible, treating the family unit while working individually with various family members. Essentially, family treatment involves family members, and a broad definition of family and family intervention is applied in this book.

Families are made up of people who have a common history, experience a degree of emotional bonding, and engage in shared goals and activities. Family issues and concerns may include physical survival, social protection, education, and development. They may involve acceptance, nurturance, approval, belonging, identity, support, and growth of individual family members. The members may or may not be biologically related, and the bonds that unite them may or may not be legal ties. Theirs is a shared experience marked by the social and psychological interdependence that is characteristic of all family relationships. The family must also be seen within the context of other systems they interact with such as those of the community, school, work, church, culture, race, social class, and beliefs.

The very notion of family conjures up memories, feelings, and experiences for each of us. Everyone has a different definition and a different family experience. Here are the defining characteristics used in this book:

- Families share a sense of history.
- Families have some degree of emotional bonding.
- Families engage in direction and goals for the future.
- Families may or may not be biologically related.
- Families may or may not have legal ties.

The bonds between family members are powerful, existing through time and often with long-term significance. Most family systems contain members who are biologically related and bound in some form of legal contract. Other family systems whose commitments are firm, whose goals are defined, and who share a sense of history are interdependent but may not be legally or biologically related. Family members may have a broad definition of who constitutes their family. Knowing whom the various members consider to be their family is important for the practitioner.

Successful families depend on individuals and the family unit to fulfill the social and psychological needs of the group as a whole and of the individual members. When families are unable to successfully reach this goal or parts of the goal, the practitioner, as an intervener, can provide an important service.

## Family Context

Helping families does not involve only the family unit. This unit must be placed in a broader context, and that context includes you as the helping practitioner. Your experience with your own family and your opinions and beliefs will affect how you relate to the families who come to you for help. It is essential, therefore, that you spend some time learning about yourself before you start working with families. In addition to having self-knowledge, you must be prepared to deal with areas that can be troubling in their ambiguity. Among the issues that arise in working with families are those that pose ethical concerns. Given the influence that practitioners have on families, they must approach ethical decisions in practice very carefully, drawing on theories of ethics, codes of professional conduct, family practice theory, cultural context, their professional identity, and public policy guidelines. Ethics and self-understanding are both involved in the way you present to others and the way you understand yourself and others. The inner dimensions of who you are affect your professional practice and lead to a number of implications regarding your interactions with families and the context of professional practice. For example, how do you effectively work with families who present spiritual ideas and religious beliefs that are different from yours, or that may even conflict with your own belief systems?

Personal and professional values and ethical standards are important in understanding who you are. Perhaps you have not given much thought to what values you hold and how these values affect the way you will practice with families. Values are those principles and standards of conduct that you deem to be good, right, or desirable. These ideals are embedded in your communication, behavior, or interaction with families. They are part of the social norms you acquire and include culturally guided likes and dislikes that are part of you. Every time you think in terms of "should," the behavior you are considering is based on a value or norm. Values may be personal to you, part of the dominant culture, or drawn from your ethnic, racial, or specific community or cultural group belief system. Values come also from your professional affiliation and education. The purpose of understanding yourself and your values is to understand how these ideals influence your thinking and behavior with families. They also influence the way families experience you; therefore, they cannot be viewed in isolation from the context of family systems.

Family assessment involves determining, with the family, their strengths and concerns. This means you must attempt to understand the behavior of family members as a family system within the context of your profession, the practice setting that employs you, and your personal values, ethics, and family system. Ethical standards are the system of moral prescriptions or ways of acting that express your values. These standards will guide you as you work with families.

## Beliefs, Preferences, and Facts

Beliefs are *assumptions* about what is true or false and may or may not be testable (Gibbs & Gambrill 1999). Assumptions guide your personal actions and shape your thinking; they are an expression of your convictions. Preferences speak to your *values* about many issues and are not a matter of determining what is right or wrong, true or false. Facts, on the other hand, are subject to evaluation and testing and a have scientific basis or other evidence-supported claim. Critical reflection provides a way for you to consider your beliefs and preferences and separate this information from the facts. The benefits of critical thinking include learning about alternatives and enhancing the quality of your decision-making skills in working with families (Gibbs & Gambrill, 1999). Such reflection allows you to discard irrelevant, misleading, and inappropriate sources of information that may be harmful to families.

When assessing family distress and functioning, you have five major ethical and value-based sources to consult. These areas are (1) personal beliefs, (2) family beliefs, (3) professional beliefs, (4) practice setting beliefs, and (5) legal requirements. Each of these carries certain obligations that should be familiar to you before you work with families.

### Personal Beliefs

Practitioners who are involved with parents and children bring their own experiences and biases to their work. They will be immersed in family matters at both the personal or subjective levels and the professional or more objective levels. By examining your personal beliefs or views and underlying assumptions about children, parents, and families, you will have a framework within which you can compare your own values and the various ways others think about the often value-laden area of child care and family life. Beliefs also influence your views of family functioning, family distress, and choice of intervention strategies as well as how you define successful outcomes for the family and/or individual family members. Your personal beliefs may additionally affect your willingness to comply with the policies of your practice setting and with professional standards of conduct and ethical practice.

A major reason for examining your personal beliefs before working with families is to identify potentially biased attitudes and behavior in yourself that may become barriers to family work. Problems of families often bring practitioners face to face with family behaviors and attitudes that have brought harm to them or others. In examining your underlying assumptions about children, parents, and families, consider the "shoulds" you have about children and parents. For example, where child abuse has occurred, a parent says, "Whipping a child is good for him. How else will he learn?" You, on the other hand, have seen the resulting marks on the child and ask yourself, "Should this child remain in the home?" While your personal beliefs and values suggest the child will be harmed if corporal punishment is continually used, legislation and policy will guide your decision, and despite your personal beliefs, leaving the child in the family unit may entitle the family to primary support services and other interventions.

Self-understanding involves examining your own family context, for it is in the context of family that you form many of your values and ethical stances. Keeping personal feelings and needs separate from professional relations, is necessary to avoid negatively impacting the families that you help. You must ask whether your personal values create barriers for working with particular families or particular problems of families and whether they affect your choice of intervention strategies. Practice models vary according to who is held responsible for problems and/or who is responsible for the solutions, and your values may affect your preference for one or another model. For example, empowerment models of intervention focus on solution aspects but not necessarily on responsibility for problem creation. Collaborative approaches will be more comfortable for those families and practitioners who perceive each other as partners in solving problems and where strengths and competence are kept in the forefront. For other situations, families and/or practitioners may be more comfortable with an "expert" model of intervention, such as those based on the medical model, particularly when serious and persistent mental health issues are evident.

Family problems and solutions are complex, and strategies for combating them should not be based only on personal preferences. Interventions must be guided by evidence-supported studies from the field. This is information derived from rigorous evaluations of intervention studies reported in peer-reviewed literature for a particular problem. Best practice interventions can also include promising practices not yet scientifically proven but recommended by community "experts." Part of your assessment process with families will be to assess your options based on the best information currently available from both the literature and the practices that meet the community's and family's needs and objectives.

Values or beliefs influence how practitioners interpret the family's problems. That is, practitioners' assumptions about the causes and change potential of the family's problems can shape their intervention planning. How practitioners respond to family problems, as well as issues of confidentiality, family self-determination, family structure, and truth-telling are influenced by personal and professional ethics, values, and obligations. Continue to monitor personal feelings about the individuals and families you are working with to ensure that you do not impede them in moving toward their goals.

## Family Beliefs

Family values and beliefs refer to the ideas, opinions, and assumptions held by individuals and families. Values and beliefs are unique to each individual and family. Although a family may share values and attitudes with the dominant culture and specific subcultures with which they identify, how they express or translate these values within their own family will be specific to the family. Cultural genograms and ecomaps (see Chapter 4) will provide you with initial tools to assess family beliefs. Exploring family rules and traditions will give you more in-depth knowledge of the family belief system. Asking questions of family members about the "shoulds" held by the family will help you access family rules concerning discipline, structure, and communication. Discussing support networks with a family helps you learn about the nature of exchanges the family members have with others outside their immediate unit.

In working with families, you may seek solutions within their belief system framework or you may work to change or shift some values where harm or safety issues are obvious. This is a delicate undertaking and must be approached with diligence and care. You as the intervener are in a position to influence family behavior and beliefs, and you must guard against imposing your own beliefs. Contracting and setting specific objectives must be agreed upon with the family before attempting any change.

## Professional Beliefs

The common base of social work values or professional beliefs has been written about extensively and can be synthesized under the following principles:

- Respect the individual worth and dignity of families.
- Value the individual's and family's capacity for change while remaining respectful of the family's right to self-determination.
- As a professional, recognize that family empowerment is a highly valued objective. This enables families to access needed information, services, and resources through equal opportunity and meaningful participation in decision making.
- Confidentiality is paramount although there are limits to confidentiality that must be a part of informed consent.
- Informed consent documents are an integral part of contracting with families. Behaving in a trustworthy manner is required.
- Practice within your areas of competence and expertise. Accountability to families and the profession must be observed. (Gambrill, 1997; Reamer, 1995)

All activities during assessment, planning and evaluation must be rooted in professional values that will allow you to offer service to families with a maximum of skill and respect while tailoring interventions to their unique needs. Professional values help us to avoid stereotyping families based on certain characteristics or consumer groups while appreciating their differences.

## Practice Setting Beliefs

Values held by agencies and organizations influence such factors as the practice setting's mission, policies, and procedures. These in turn will directly affect who is served and how. Policies regarding eligibility for service greatly impact program and case decision levels. Personal and professional values may conflict with practice setting directives, especially in areas of service priorities and program development. The practice setting culture and even physical arrangements reflect organizational values. For example, a cramped and cluttered space or the lack of available evening appointment times may give families a sense that they are not valued. The amount of autonomy staff are given in making decisions with families will be reflected in how decisions are made. Empowered practitioners may feel better able to facilitate family empowerment.

## Legal Requirements

All jurisdictions in North America have legal requirements regarding limits to confidentiality. You will need to know and explain to families, as part of the original contracting for services, that confidentiality may not apply in all instances—such as reporting child abuse, reporting the potential of a family member to harm self or others, and responding to a court order requesting family records. Other regulations may also be in effect, such as managed care policies concerning documentation for services. You need to learn what legal and licensing regulations you work under for ethical documentation of family practice.

# Maintaining Ethical Standards

Beyond professional and legal regulations, practitioners must take care in how they use information because of their potential power and influence with families. The pressure to make ethical judgments can indeed be overwhelming, not only for students and novices but also for skilled and experienced practitioners. Two major issues will be considered in this section: (1) the importance of ethical decision making, and (2) confidentiality and the application of ethical principles to practice dilemmas.

## Ethical Decision-Making Protocol

Practitioners need to develop an awareness of and sensitivity to ethical decision making. Tensions between personal beliefs and the profession's espoused values may create ethical dilemmas for practitioners. These tensions underlie many ethical practice decisions and dilemmas. There are no simple answers to these situations and there is no agreement on whether personal or professional values should take precedence. When values conflict, practitioners must weigh their competing obligations to the family, the employer, the profession, and third parties against the requirements of their own conscience on a case-by-case basis. Practitioners must continually examine the nature of their personal beliefs as well as the ways in which those values influence their understanding of family problems, system problems, the application of knowledge, and strategies for intervention.

You need to keep in mind families' rights and well-being as you make decisions based on the ethics of the profession. Remember, ethical action includes commission (what was done) and omission (what was not done). Failing to act may be overlooked when you are assessing a course of action. Ethical decisions must be made in a rational manner that is comprehensible to others, including families, colleagues, employers, and professional associations.

Despite careful planning, ethical conflicts will arise. Gambrill (1997) and Reamer (1995) discuss at length the importance of ethical thinking and actions. The following protocol, based on their work, can guide ethical decision making.

**Guideline 1: Describe accurately what the issue or dilemma is.**

- What values or ethics are in conflict?
- Who is involved in the dilemma and in what ways do interests conflict?

- What theory and facts do you have about human behavior that can be applied to your understanding of the situation?
- What evidence-supported knowledge do you have about the problems to help you plan interventions?
- What personal values and biases do you hold concerning the family and the family's situation? Identify your values and biases as well as the ethics of your profession to avoid imposing personal values on the family or the family situation.

**Guideline 2: Describe potential courses of action or inaction.**

- What alternatives are available to you and the family? Identify alternative action plans with the family.
- What are the alternative options and their consequences? Consider potential "unintended" consequences.
- What are the pros and cons of each alternative identified? Weigh the pros and cons of each alternative with the family.

**Guideline 3: Consider the criteria by which you will judge the merits of each option.**

- Is there a hierarchy of values to employ?
- Have you discussed these with other staff, supervisors, or other practice setting administrators and legal consultants?

**Guideline 4: Choose the option that you think is best using your decision-making criteria.**

- What alternative is the most ethical to pursue? Explain your reasons for selecting this course of action or inaction.
- Is this a well-reasoned argument based on appropriate consultation and in consideration of the five sources of ethical knowledge (self, family, profession, practice setting, and legal regulations)?
- Implement the plan that you, with the family, have determined to be the most positive and the most ethical.

Use of this protocol becomes necessary when several ethical guidelines conflict and thus the potential solutions are imperfect and often unsatisfactory. Sometimes dilemmas can be avoided through careful planning and good assessment procedures. For example, use clear and understandable language to inform families of the purpose of proposed services as well as the risks related to them. Some examples are limits to available services, relevant costs, reasonable alternatives to service, appeal procedures, and families' right to refuse or withdraw from treatment; these must be presented to families during the engagement process.

Pratitioners' standards of practice, knowledge, and skills are the foundation of ethical practice. Careful application will help practitioners avoid potentially serious situations, such as the following:

1. Misdiagnosing the seriousness of an adolescent's depression, which could lead to the young person's suicide.

2. Underevaluating the potential of further assault by a violence-prone partner in supporting a woman's decision to remain in a highly dangerous domestic situation.

3. Making an incorrect assessment of an adoptive home leading to an adoption breakdown and subsequent maladaptive behaviors for the child involved.

4. Making an error in judgment that leaves an infant in a situation where abuse might occur, leading to the child's serious injury or death.

In such contexts, quality of service and quality of care must be maintained so that a situation of unethical conduct or incompetence is avoided.

## Confidentiality Concerns

Historically, professionals such as social workers and others have developed guidelines to assist practitioners in making sound, ethical decisions. National bodies such as the National Association of Social Workers (NASW) have developed codes of ethics. These codes are written to address practice settings, practice issues, and problems that practitioners face every day. The codes do not prescribe explicitly the professional behavior required. Often, competency guidelines are developed to provide more detailed descriptions of professional behavior to be used in various settings for reasonable practice. Specific conduct in specific circumstances is often required, as noted in the following discussion of common concerns.

*Legal Obligations*   The limits of confidentiality, as when a practitioner has a legal obligation to report a situation, even against the family's wishes, need to be spelled out clearly to families at the onset of contact. Do not wait until a crisis arises. Stress to the clients that confidentiality cannot be maintained under conditions outlined in legal statutes or when there are compelling professional reasons for breaking it. State these conditions in the first contact with families. Examples include laws mandating the reporting of child abuse, child neglect, and elder abuse. The limits of confidentiality must be described to the family with assurance that confidentiality will be maintained unless there are concerns about harm or safety.

*Fully Informing Families*   Families have a right to truthful information about matters relevant to their treatment and welfare. They should be fully informed about assessment methods, and any interventions selected need to reflect the outcomes the family wants. Families should receive clear descriptions of the cost, time, and effort involved in the treatment process (Gibbs & Gambrill, 1999).

*Obligation to Adhere to Regulations*   The desire to protect families from harm may raise some issues related to paternalism in social work. Forcing a family to accept services against its wishes is an example of paternalism. Protecting families from themselves when they fail to exercise "good" judgment raises concerns about self-determination and informed consent. Sometimes the practitioner believes that harm to the family may result if the helper adheres to policies and regulations. Examples of this may include the legal mandate to report child abuse, or practice setting policy to report income or assets for determining the level of services or the costs of services. The issue is one of protecting the family's welfare and deciding whether this justifies not adhering to legal requirements or practice setting policies.

*Service Limitations*    Once you have decided what services the family requires, you will face considerations about the types of services, the duration, and intensity of services needed. You will likely make these decisions based on the family's needs, ability to pay, or other criteria, such as needs for growth, change, safety, and stability. Most families benefit from a set of integrated services tailored to their individual needs, so multiple interventions may be required.

Practitioners may face different kinds of dilemmas in managed care agencies or in organizations that have constraints on the amount of services they can offer. Many publicly funded agencies are limited in the support or services they can provide because of financial constraints. Therefore, hard choices must be made as to the number of families served and the way these families are selected. Sometimes practitioners may disagree with agency decisions when they believe services are denied to families they see as being in great need. What then? What do practitioners do? They cannot serve families who are not approved for services by the practitioner's employing agency. Do they try to change the decision at the agency level? These are ethical dilemmas for the practitioner.

Coordinating multiple interventions is more likely to address a number of needs and will stand a better chance of making a difference to the family than will a single intervention. This makes sense from the ecological and systems perspective as well as from the point of view of service provision, particularly when service constraints are present, and the practitioner is able to develop formal, professional services with less traditional resources. The practitioner's willingness to ensure an appropriate response to the family that is unique to their needs and priorities should serve as the practice guideline when both services and opportunities are limited.

## Summary Of Key Practice Principles

Making ethical decisions and dealing with ethical dilemmas are necessary elements of day-to-day family practice. Practitioners must constantly monitor themselves to ensure that their personal values do not create barriers for them in working with particular families or particular family problems. This means that part of the assessment process with families is to assess your values, beliefs, and preferences regarding the family you are working with against the facts of the family's situation for understanding the planned change processes. This knowledge—of yourself and the family you are helping—combined with the agency values, professional standards, and legal requirements, should guide your decisions. The following factors need to be considered in ethical decision making.

- Family's interests, rights, and values
- The interests and rights of others involved in the situation (e.g., individual family members versus the family system)
- Your professional code of ethics and how this relates to the situation

- Your personal values and ethical stance
- Practice setting policies and procedures that relate to the situation
- The legal and licensing regulations and implications of each intervention decision (Gambrill, 1997).

Gibbs and Gambrill (1999, p. 190) provide a checklist of ethical concerns that may help guide your ethical decision making. See Figure 1.1 on page 14.

## Learning Activities

### Activity 1.1: What should I do?

1. First, read the instructions and then complete the task presented below on your own. When you have completed this activity, share responses with your classmates and discuss the similarities and differences of your responses.
2. Discuss when you first heard these ideas with the class.

The task is to consider the following situations. Think carefully about your views and beliefs about the practice concerns and pay special attention to any "shoulds" that arise. Complete the following sentences:

1. Single-parent families should always_____
2. Single-parent families should never _____
3. Same-sex partner families should always _____
4. Same-sex partner families should never _____
5. Children who have behavior or conduct problems should always _____
6. Families using corporal punishment with children should always _____
7. Families using corporal punishment with children should never _____

### Activity 1.2: My Family Journal
### My Family Experience: Beliefs and Preferences

Think about your family and your family experiences. Family experiences influence and shape your beliefs and preferences. Write your responses to the following questions in the spaces provided below and then discuss your responses with classmates. Self-understanding involves examining your family experiences. It is in the context of family experiences that you draw your values and ethical stances.

What are the "shoulds" derived from your family that you learned as a child? Think about your own family experience and the role it played in creating your values, beliefs, preferences, attitudes, and biases. Describe how your family experience influenced you and give an example:

a) Your attitudes and values:

b) Your beliefs about families:

c) Your biases about families:

d) The influence of your family experience on your thinking and practice with families:

---

A. Keeping Confidentiality
  1. Limits on confidentiality are described.
  2. Confidentiality is maintained unless there are concerns about harm to others.
B. Selecting Objectives
  3. Objectives focused on result in real-life gains for clients.
  4. Objectives are related to the key concerns of clients.
C. Selecting Methods
  5. Assessment methods relied on provide accurate, relevant information.
  6. Intervention methods selected are likely to attain outcomes that clients value.
  7. Assessment, intervention, and evaluation methods are acceptable to clients and to significant others.
D. Fully Informing Clients
  8. Clients are given an accurate description of the accuracy of assessment methods used.
  9. Clients receive accurate estimates of the likely success of recommended procedures.
  10. Alternative methods and their likely consequences are described.
  11. Clear descriptions of the cost, time, and effort involved in a suggested method are presented in language intelligible to clients.
  12. An accurate description and the likelihood of side effects (both positive and negative) of suggested services are provided.
  13. An accurate description of the helper's competence to offer needed services is provided.
  14. Appropriate arrangements are made to involve others in decisions when clients cannot give informed consent.
E. Being Competent
  15. Helpers are competent to use the assessment measures they rely on.
  16. Helpers are competent to use the intervention methods they rely on.
F. Being Accountable
  17. Arrangements are made for ongoing feedback about progress using valid progress indictors.
G. Encouraging a Culture of Thoughtfulness
  18. Positive feedback is provided to colleagues for the critical evaluation of claims and arguments.
  19. Efforts are made to change agency procedures and policies that decrease the likelihood of providing evidence-based practice.

**Figure 1.1** Checklist of Ethical Concerns (*Source: From* Critical Thinking for Social Workers: Exercises for the Helping Professions, *Revised Edition, by L. Gibbs and E. Gambrill, p. 190. Copyright © 1999 Pine Forge Press. Reprinted by permission.*)

## Activity 1.3: Case Study
## Applying Ethical Decision Making

*Instructions:* First read the Yellowbird Family Case Study (Chapter 11). Then (1) describe the ethical conflicts in the case and (2) suggest how these might be handled. These examples are not exhaustive but are meant to serve as a starting point from which to explore things further.

1. Describe a confidentiality dilemma in the case.
2. Is the value of self-determination relevant to this case, and if so how?
3. Identify the values and beliefs about how this family operates or functions.
4. Are there competing values in this case? Describe these.
5. Identify other situations that may involve competing personal and professional values dilemmas.
6. In class, role-play for 15 minutes the first meeting with the Yellowbird Family and present the issue of confidentiality. Then complete the Checklist of Ethical Concerns (Gibbs & Gambrill, 1999) shown in the Summary of Key Practice Principles to be sure you address the main practice values. How well did you do? How well did your colleagues do?

# CHAPTER TWO

# Getting Started

Many books address the various aspects of conducting a family assessment. The practice aspects of conducting an assessment are the focus of this book. To enhance the quality of the assessment process and findings, you must accept three guidelines for gathering information about a family and its members: (1) Good assessment information results from a planned or systematic approach to the family and the family situation. (2) To make profound changes in the life of an individual, child or family, the most effective strategy engages the family unit in the process. Family systems thinking and planning are necessary when change is needed in the environment (Huffman, Mehlinger, & Kerivan, 2000). (3) Family experiences play a critical role in causing, promoting, or reinforcing behaviors and competencies in family members (Corcoran, 2000). For example, children with early cognitive, social, and behavioral difficulties are known to have increased rates of conduct problems through their teenage years. Understanding this will allow us to examine the child's early behaviors within the environmental context that put this child at risk for getting off track in school, with peer relationships, and with self-control. Starting with these assumptions will help you to organize your thinking for the kinds of questions that are likely to effect change in the family. The assumptions with which practitioners view the child, family, and environment will set the theoretical framework for thinking about resources for intervention and change.

# Families and Environments

To understand the complexities of the family's environment and situation, practitioners will need a guiding framework that provides direction and focus for practice (Rothery, 1999). Viewing the family in the context of their environments is important if you are to learn how families, individuals, and environments change. The environment where the child and family develop informs us about their supports, emerging competencies, stresses, and needs. Examining environments the family interacts with informs us about their adaptation to stresses, needs, and problems. Focusing on environments where individuals and families develop and interact is identified as a multisystem perspective. This perspective offers an opportunity to examine or assess the adequacy of the many relationships that link individuals with their environments (Rothery, 1999).

Thinking from a multisystem perspective about family assessment and intervention is a sound and effective way to approach the family's unique situation. Each family system will have its own developmental pattern and interactional system. Common patterns can be identified but essentially family systems are distinctive in their own ways. Thinking in a multisystem framework is the first step to getting started and determining creative approaches to family circumstances. It is also necessary to have family involvement to ensure that appropriate resources and interventions are connected to the problem-solving process. Solutions must fit the family situation. Engaging the family at the very beginning gives you the best opportunity to systematically and comprehensively respond to the diversity of family need.

How will you know the family is involved and engaged in problem solving? There are sophisticated scales to measure family engagement (Alexander & Luborsky, 1986), but for the beginning practitioner, evidence of family engagement can be seen as family members attending meetings with the practitioner, participating in meetings, relating or feeling connected to the practitioner, participating toward the helping goals and objectives, and adopting the contract for service (M. Macgowan, personal communication). The nature and quality of family involvement will vary depending on many factors, but it is necessary to examine how each family is organized and functioning to understand how they are involved and engaged in the process of change.

# Thinking About Families

Family life and family functioning are incredibly complex processes and cannot be understood through a single observation or encounter. Consider the following example: If you look at a photograph of a family engaged in an activity such as playing a game, watching TV, or eating a meal, what could you say about the people? Although you would have only a snapshot of data, you could say a great deal about what you think you know. The difficulty, however, is that you may misinterpret what you see because of viewing that family from your own life experiences, events, values, cultural beliefs, and personal and professional knowledge. Depending on your point of view, values, or theoretical understanding, you can make many statements based on that photograph, but they will be only conjecture or hypothesizing built on limited information. It is a good place to start, but there is a great deal more to learn since a family in action, sitting with you, can provide far more information in terms of both the family interactions and their processes. As a practitioner, you need to make sense of the complex information, and understanding the dynamic interplay of families as a system helps reduce the complexity.

Whether novice or expert in working with families, you can begin to make guesses or hypotheses about what it might be like to be a part of the family grouping in that photograph. From looking at it, you might say the family members appear loving, lonely, or distant from each other by noting their physical position and emotional or facial expressions. You might note whether individuals are touching, holding, or gesturing to another. However, you are still just making assumptions based on that one moment in time. What you infer about the family will to a large extent be influenced by how you think and what you are thinking.

Other sources of information are necessary. Knowledge of family functioning is needed to extend your understanding of what is happening. Knowledge about family theory is another source, as is knowledge about your own family experiences. Potentially, all knowledge sources are helpful. And importantly, the knowledge, skills, values, and attitudes related to your thinking affect your practice decisions with families. Being aware of what you know, don't know, and need to know helps you reflect on your actions.

Gibbs and Gambrill (1999, p. 4) address the importance of critical thinking for practice decisions. Critical thinking shapes the thinking and doing of the assessment and intervention process. The following questions can help you evaluate your initial thinking about a family:

- What assumptions am I making about this family?
- What am I taking for granted about this family?
- What data, facts, information, and observations am I using to arrive at my point of view about this family?
- How am I interpreting the information about this family?
- What conclusions am I coming to about this family?

Practitioners use many kinds of criteria to evaluate what they think and see and the course of action they will take. Recognizing cognitive biases will help you avoid making unsound practice decisions. Awareness can keep you from accepting initial assumptions without question or believing that causes are similar to their effects (Gibbs & Gambrill, 1999). Being aware of the sources of information or knowledge helps you avoid reaching wrong conclusions about a family and their situation.

## Family Engagement

Families who seek the services of a practitioner or social worker vary greatly as will the kinds of issues they want help for and the type of change desired. Some of the ways they will differ include family structure, developmental life stage, ethnicity, race, and their functional abilities due to the nature of their troubles and troubling behaviors. Some families require considerable help while others need less. Some will ask for service while others will not be as forthcoming and may even be referred by the court to you. Regardless of the types of services or issues families are seeking help with, they want to know that you are competent to design interventions to help solve their problems.

Engaging the family in the process of change is paramount. The focus of concern with a family begins with the practitioner's behavior and the family's response. A relationship is needed between the two systems and this connecting of the practitioner with the family system is referred to as "joining the family" or the therapeutic alliance. It is an alliance and connection of the two systems, not just the individuals. All members of this joined system can influence the change process. Therefore, the first encounters are very important and will determine the nature and process of what evolves and unfolds in the helping relationship.

Through this helping relationship the practitioner begins to develop an understanding and complete, coherent story of a family and its struggles and demands. That is, what is the current situation and what is needed to make a difference for the family? Relationship building engages the family so the practitioner can build a knowledge base for understanding how a family responds to demands from the various environments as well as providing ideas about what supports it needs. The basis for helping to reduce the complexity is to understand families as social systems who are interacting with multiple systems—both among the family members and between the family members and others. The resulting information helps us decide what intervention is needed to generate particular results (Corcoran, 2000; Rothery & Enns, 2001; Weiss, 1995).

Social workers interview families in practically every type of organization and environment and work with a variety of family structures, problems, and issues. Each of these settings will have somewhat different criteria for engaging families and conducting family interviews as well as different data or information to be collected. There are, however, common elements in family assessment that apply regardless of the setting or the mandate for service.

## Guiding Principles of Assessment

Deciding what intervention to use grows directly from assessment. Consequently, a number of issues need to be considered about the assessment process. Culture and beliefs of the agency, the practitioner, and the family influence every aspect of practice and must be reflected in assessment and intervention choices. A frequently encountered difficulty is that many families seeking help come from backgrounds and experiences different from those of practitioners and social workers, and this may make family engagement for service a formidable task. As a first and most important step, practitioners must recognize the need for sensitive and responsive assessment approaches. Second, they must understand the purpose, key concepts, and assumptions of family functioning.

## Sensitive and Responsive Assessment

Social workers and other practitioners have an obligation to attend to issues of quality in assessment, using sound theoretical frameworks, systematic approaches to interviewing, and standardized instruments and techniques to gather data. Also, they must always be aware of where good assessment leads: to interventions that are appropriate for addressing the family's problems and that have good prospects for producing positive outcomes. Therefore, practitioners must be mindful of the assessment process. The following thoughts should help set this context.

1. Families have the right to receive the most effective available service to prevent or reduce distress and improve functioning. This requires practitioners to keep abreast of the current intervention research on outcome effectiveness (Tutty, 1990).

2. When family assessment is well defined and when interventions are based on current best evidence from scientific research supporting the use of a certain treatment or intervention, the outcome is more likely to be positive (Corcoran, 1992; Gibbs & Gambrill, 1999; Thomlison, 1984).

3. Clients should be offered as a first choice treatment, interventions with some significant degree of empirical support, where such knowledge exists, and only provided other treatments after such first choice treatment have been given a legitimate trial and shown not to be efficacious (Thyer & Wodarski, 1998, p. 16).

4. No one study, no matter how carefully done or how positive the results, is considered evidence by itself. A group of well-done studies with similar findings is needed to come to the conclusion that there is good evidence for a particular approach (Hughes, 1999).

5. It is best to focus on characteristics of individuals and families that are prosocial, resilient, or adaptive, those that are generally regarded as competencies rather than pathologies. Social skills, communication, and learning styles are promising targets of intervention and lend themselves to enhancement (Fantuzzo, McDermott, & Lutz, 1999).

6. Sensitive and responsive assessment requires practitioners to widen the scope of their assessment to attend to the various developmental and ecological factors with greater precision for more culturally diverse populations (Fantuzzo, McDermott, & Lutz, 1999).

7. Assessment needs to be taken at multiple points in time to develop an adequate understanding of supports and resources for intervention for diverse populations, such as highly stressed and low-income families and those who are at disproportionate risk for victimization (Ammerman & Hersen, 1999).

For beginning practitioners, assessment can seem overwhelming, but families deserve to receive the best assessment and intervention strategy available. The broader your knowledge base, the better able you will be to provide this. The knowledge base underlying the multisystemic framework is supported by good research evidence as well as expert opinion (Henggeler, Schoenwald, Bordin, Rowland, & Cunningham, 1998). Therefore, multisystemic core concepts form a sound basis for assessment and intervention for families and family circumstances.

## Elements of Assessment

The importance of high-quality assessment is underscored by today's practice context, where service tends toward time-limited, brief treatments and evidence-supported practice, incorporating family-centered approaches. It is therefore essential for practitioners to view the goal of assessment as a brief strategy that is comprehensive and systematically focused and that views evaluation as essential (Corcoran, 1992; Thyer & Wodarski, 1998). The ultimate goal of assessment will be to make resource and intervention decisions that address family functioning and the environments impacting the lives of families. The framework for assessment should be open to change as new information is presented or new situations emerge.

*Purpose of Assessment* Assessment is done to determine family resources or strengths in order to address the family concerns. Making sense of data through assessment has three specific functions:

1. *Understanding the family issues.* Assessment provides a framework for defining and conceptualizing family issues although it can never explain all family phenomena. Assessment informs you about the family's adaptive responses to the stresses and demands in the environment.

2. *Planning for interventions.* Assessment assists the practitioner in organizing and synthesizing family information to provide a focus for intervention. Developing understanding of the linkages and interdependent relationships the family has with other systems provides a picture of how much each of these systems affects the other. The appropriateness of a specific intervention to address the family's stresses and demands can then be determined. Strengthening the formal and informal supports in the lives of families is then possible.

3. *Identifying needed family supports and resources.* Assessment provides a framework to identify what outcomes are desired. Clearly, exploring with the family their need for support and resources improves outcomes of service. Rothery (1999; Rothery & Enns, 2001) has identified four general areas in which families may need supports and resources.
   - *Concrete, instrumental support*—basic goods, material, and financial aspects necessary to cope with everyday demands of life. Finding adequate accommodation, child care, or items such as a refrigerator focus on such needs. Formal agencies and/or extended family and friends are possible resources for these needs.
   - *Information, knowledge and skills*—information and knowledge that families need if they are to make informed decisions about options or alternatives available to them. Examples are information about parenting a child with troubling behaviors, preparing for employment, caring for a child's medical condition, or leaving a violent partner. Educational programs are a source of formal assistance, while peers, family, colleagues, and friends can be informal resources to address this type of need.

- *Emotional supports*—important to daily functioning. If these relationships are maladaptive, absent, or stressed, then families do not feel supported, understood, or safe. Counseling that focuses on therapeutic relationships will be required if family members are to change their experiences.
- *Affiliational supports*—important to provide families with a sense of belonging in the neighborhood, family network, and community. The opportunity to have meaningful social roles is necessary for validation. Friends and relatives are important in this area.

Exploring these four areas of support and how they are reflected in the family's circumstances provides the initial information for framing a family's situation and experiences. Through the interviewing process, you and the family learn about the behavior and social functioning of the children and the family in their environmental context and discover and highlight their strengths and concerns. This entails a process of fact finding and organizing information about the issues and concerns of the family. The use of interviews and other assessment tools will be used to collect this information about the family concerns, strengths, and functioning. Assessment is viewed both as an ongoing process and a product (Hepworth, Rooney, & Larsen, 1997).

*The Assessment Process*   The assessment process includes gathering, analyzing, and synthesizing relevant data about the child and family context not only to identify the stresses and resulting adaptation to the stresses and problems, but also to evaluate strengths and resources. The setting, the family's problems, and the practitioner's role and orientation to the information collection task will determine the nature of the assessment process. Emphasis is on discovering strengths. The practitioner will look for characteristics that are prosocial—positive coping skills; resilient or adaptive skills; ways the family has deployed problem-solving abilities in previous situations. These are family competencies and strengths that can move the family toward effective outcomes. Focusing on the social skills, communication methods, and learning styles of the family is often wise, since they lend themselves relatively easily to positive change (Corcoran, 2000; Fantuzzo, McDermott, & Lutz, 1997).

As mentioned earlier, building a relationship with family members is essential if the practitioner is to obtain high-quality information. At the beginning of family contact, rapport is established through the interview process. Practitioners will require effective communication skills to accomplish this. Apart from the reasons a family is seeking assistance, families must be active participants in the change process, but seeking help is not easy for most people. Talking about your private family troubles to a stranger creates anxieties about what will happen. Families will be worried about how you will view them and their current reactions to stresses and difficulties. They will also be concerned about your thoughts and reactions to their differences from you in gender, class, race, and cultural practices. The practitioner's tone of acceptance in this initial contact is critical to establishing rapport and building the necessary relationship and alliance with the family.

The most credible information will be obtained by interviewing the family in their natural environments. Assessing the family in their home environment provides an opportunity to observe their interactions within that context. It will diminish, but not alleviate, the family reactions, anxieties, and feelings about help. Assessing families in an office places them in an unfamiliar setting in which to interact with you. In the home context you can see the impact of problems on the family and the influence of family interaction and relationships on the problems. Interviewing in the family home gives you access to the interaction of people, places, times, and contexts that are the sources and the solutions of family functioning (Bronfenbrenner, 1986; Whittaker, Schinke, & Gilchrist, 1986). Home visit strategies have been identified as especially effective in addressing various parenting and parent-child health, social, and emotional problems. Early family support and education interventions have shown evidence of positive impact, particularly with families of young children.

Therefore, to understand a family's functioning, it is essential to use assessment strategies that take into account the individuals and the environments influencing them. Furthermore, the context in which a family is functioning determines whether this functioning is adaptive or maladaptive. The impact of culture is an example; language barriers or different cultural meanings of a particular situation can have varied interpretations if viewed outside the family home and neighborhood. These issues are particularly salient when assessing parent and child concerns. Parental expectations of children's behavior vary by neighborhood and ethnicity (Fantuzzo, McDermott, & Lutz, 1999), and expectations influence perceptions and interpretations of children's behaviors. For example, families living in violent neighborhoods are more likely to encourage children to defend themselves physically, and this increases their aggressive behavior. Often, a practitioner's assessment of behavior or interactions will be much more accurate if the family is observed in its natural context.

The developmental-ecological perspective emphasizes the importance of human development in the context in which the development occurs, and seeks to understand human development in terms of changes over time (Cicchetti & Lynch, 1993). The situation must be understood within the context of the dynamic and continuous development—was it typical or atypical? This reflects the adaptation or maladaption of various behaviors in individuals and families.

*Assessment Tools* Assessment tools are used to gather pertinent information about a family. Some are more complex and advanced than others and require considerable skill and knowledge about a specific area. An example of an assessment tool used by advanced practitioners is the *Diagnostic and Statistical Manual for Mental Disorders (DSM-IV)* (American Psychiatric Association, 1994) used for a clinical diagnosis in mental health of adults and children. Other methods and tools require less skill. Although there is a need for high-quality assessment information to inform intervention strategies, beginning practitioners should use those tools geared to their skill and competence level, moving to the more sophisticated methods and measures as their skill increases.

Assessment strategies vary but all family assessment processes should take into account how children, adults, and families function in their multiple and simultaneous environments—how they interact and experience each situation. The type of assessment will affect outcome. There will be a variation between qualitative and quantitative assessments. Children and individuals with specific difficulties will need specific assessment tools. For example, you may be interested in a parent's attitude toward a child and a child's attitude toward a parent. Tools specifically developed for this problem assessment are found in the Hudson (1982) *Clinical Measurement Package;* in Corcoran and Fischer (1994); and Jordan and Franklin's (1995) *Clinical Assessment for Social Workers.* Observation is a qualitative approach to assessment, but observation using a standardized questionnaire or checklist provides a quantitative assessment and therefore enriches the information, making it more personal. Qualitative and quantitative approaches may both be appropriate depending on the situation, the problem, and the skills of the practitioner. The practitioner treats the family as the expert on their situation, obtaining data through collaboration, respect, and cooperation.

Practitioners need to use multiple methods for obtaining data, and they should use tools that are well known and theoretically constructed. Tools help practitioners measure family functioning across settings—for example, the frequency of family conflict or the type of parental functioning—and provide a more objective assessment of a specific family problem. The findings serve as the basis for identifying the plan for change. Practitioners need to use assessment techniques in which they are skilled and which they are competent to administer. A compendium of brief assessment tools relevant for today's practice context is available in the work of Corcoran and Fischer (1994) which provides a comprehensive review of standardized measures for clinical practice. Some of the areas of family functioning that a practitioner may measure include social support, attitudes toward a child or spouse, emotional closeness, and level of stress. The tools and measures referenced are rapid assessment instruments and require only a brief time frame for administration. Beginning practitioners will probably use one or a combination of the assessment types descried here:

1. *Interviewing techniques.* Interviewing is probably the most frequently used method to gather information. Most practitioners use this qualitative form of data collection because it can readily reveal the context and meaning of the family's situation. "Interviewing is a highly personal, interpretive, reflective, and elaborative" process (Jordan & Franklin, 1995, p. 102). Questions are asked and answered, and from this interchange the practitioner extracts meaning about the family. When family members are seen as a group the practitioner can gain understanding of the family structure, dynamics, power, and interaction. Such an interview provides information about family functioning and shows the practitioner where intervention can change the patterns of the family system.

   Interviews can be structured, semistructured, or open ended. Structured interviews have formulated questions that are asked by the practitioner, and the usual procedure is to follow the set questions. Semistructured interviews also have a list of questions, but they serve as beginning points from which the practitioner can branch out, following leads suggested by the answers. Open-ended interviews do not have a predetermined set of questions and the practitioner is able to ask questions as they arise in the meeting and probe for further responses. All forms of interviews have specific purposes you must stay within.

2. *Mapping and graphic techniques.* The social support grid expands our understanding of the family's ecomap. Mapping family supports explores sources of strength and assistance and identifies critical resources and types of support available for each family member. You will identify systematically the types of concrete, instrumental, and affective supports available to help the family. Completing the social support grid with the family may give you information you can use to make the family feel more hopeful; the exercise may even uncover resources to explore further. The goal is to gather sufficient information to show the family that there is real support available in their environment, even if they have not tapped it deeply, and to mobilize encouragement for the problem-solving phase of designing the services plan. What kinds of informational, emotional, and affiliational supports are present? What is needed? These are the questions to explore in developing the social support grid. An example of the ecomap, genogram, and social network map and grid are found in Chapter 4 with a discussion of how to use these assessment tools.

   Timelines can also be used to map the critical events and conditions in the life cycle of the family or one of its members. The unit of attention for the timeline could be a child, the family, and/or events in the family. A sequence of events is chronologically organized and graphically represented through these timelines. This allows for the tracking of events over time and viewing the order in which events occurred as separate or layered.

3. *Family scales.* These are standardized measures that assess family functioning. Corcoran and Fischer (1994) provide a complete list of rapid assessment tools, including many self-anchored rating scales. Examples of family scales appear in Chapter 6.

4. *Observational techniques.* These are tasks or assignments the family completes while the practitioner observes. Family roles, power, interaction, and decision making are usually observed. Role plays or simulations are used to enact a family situation or a dyadic situation. Having members reenact a family conflict or verbal exchange between members often allows both practitioner and family to gain greater understanding of a situation or issue.

Assessment is both a process to determine the family's resources, difficulties, stressors, and reactions and an intervention in the family system. The family is viewed as the expert and is engaged to work on the chosen area of concern; in this way, a strength-based focus directs the solution.

*Writing the Assessment Report*  The product of assessment is usually a written report summarizing the family members' issues and their strengths and resources (Hepworth, Rooney & Larson, 1997). With data organized by headings, reports integrate practitioner's impressions, the information from the interview(s), and any assessment measures used to summarize family, marital, individual, and social functioning. Done properly, a report is a summary of the data obtained in the fact-finding process about individuals and family interactions and presents a rich framework for facilitating interventions to promote change. The report also includes a plan for providing resources and interventions.

The assessment report is difficult for many practitioners to write because it is not an essay but a synthesis of the data collected. An example of a family situation assessment and the assessment report can be seen in Chapter 8. You will note specific areas about the family functioning that are reported and described. The writer has synthesized the facts and impressions into a coherent description of strengths and resources, presenting the family's coping abilities individually as well as describing the environmental strengths and resources such as housing, employment, and support through social networks.

## Summary of Key Practice Principles

In practice, it is useful for practitioners to adopt a clear conceptual multisystemic framework for viewing the family and family functioning. Systemic thinking is helpful to this process because it allows the practitioner to examine data and information about family relationships that impact the family. As well, this framework helps you understand the influence of the individual and other systems on the family. Families are both the source and the solution to their problems and concerns. Identifying family strengths is an essential part of assessment. The following assumptions are key to conducting family assessment:

- Believe that each family member has potential for positive development.
- Assume that all family members have an inner competence or strength.
- Adopt the belief that all families have strengths.
- Assume that focusing on strengths leads to finding more strengths.
- Realize that family-generated solutions to problems are the ones that are most effective and long lasting (Thomlison & Thomlison, 1996).

## Learning Activities

### Activity 2.1

Divide into small groups of three or four students for a discussion of family strengths and resources. Share the results of your discussion with others when you have finished.

- Why it is important to use a strength-based approach when working with families?
- What are some of the issues that arise when using a problem-focused approach?
- Make a list of strengths you would look for in a family.
- Identify three strengths about your family.

*Activity 2.2*

Discuss family engagement and its importance in working with families.

- Which types of families are difficult to engage, and what techniques do you think may work?
- What unique characteristics do you bring to this process that facilitate family engagement? How did you learn this about yourself?
- Identify cultural variables (ethnic and professional) that may affect the quality of communication and family engagement. How would you address these challenges?

CHAPTER THREE

# *The Family System*

Afamily is probably the most basic unit to which anyone belongs. It determines nationality, ethnic group, and the kind of community in which we grow to adulthood. It plays a part in social and economic status, religious affiliation, and even occupation. It provides roots; it defines attitudes and values; and it is a large part of who we are. The ability of parents to develop a sense of security, self, and family identity for children is critical to the children's developmental outcomes. Most important perhaps, a family provides a sense of belonging. This sense of belonging shapes both attitudes and behavior. Individual outcomes, as a result of good-quality family care, show the impact that continuity of family relationships and attachments have on one's developmental history. When one or both parents raise a child over a continuous period of time, providing him or her with good physical, social, and emotional care, that child feels loved and valued.

Intervention is influenced by views held about families, by both the practitioner and the family. Practitioners have personal and professional beliefs about families (see Chapter 1) and these beliefs influence how assessment and intervention are implemented. For example, is an assessment done in the agency setting or in the family home environment? Is an intervention chosen to change the systems that interact with the family or to change a child? Is an intervention selected based on "what we know" about its effectiveness or because its use is the common practice of the agency? All of the practices are influenced by the personal, professional, and practicing beliefs of systems. Most important, families hold views about themselves and their family life, and it is difficult to address the factors that bring a family for help if the family's beliefs, attitudes, and family sense of belonging are not explored. For example, a practitioner's belief about parenting in a single-parent household may influence how he or she receives, perceives, and treats that family.

A practitioner who believes alcoholism is a consequence of personal weakness will likely respond differently to a family experiencing alcoholism than to a family experiencing the effects of a stroke, when the practitioner believes the stroke is beyond the control of the individual or family. Thinking about whom a family consists of and exploring with a family what ideas and attitudes affect the issues in the family are the beginning points of family assessment.

## Family

The family is a vastly different unit today from what it was twenty or thirty years ago. Then, the "normal" family unit consisted of a legally married man and woman living together with their mutual children—possibly with a grandparent in the household, and an uncle or aunt nearby. But today there is a vast number of other family types, all of which may consider themselves to be "normal." Many families, no matter what form they take or lifestyle they pursue, experience concerns, difficulties, and problems.

Various family structures have both liberating features and new stresses concerning choices for individuals. In the past, family roles and boundaries were relatively clear-cut and rigid. Today, family structures "mirror the openness, complexity, and diversity of our contemporary lifestyles" (Elkind, 1994, p. 1). Roles and boundaries are far more fluid and flexible now and the family is also more vulnerable to pressures from the outside than in the past. Consequently, it is important to think of families as different from the family popularized in the image of the 1950s.

The very clearly defined roles and boundaries of the idealized family—a household with two married parents and their children—was especially beneficial to children and adolescents, offering well-defined limits and standards. Children and youth could afford to focus on the demands and conflicts of growing up. This was helpful to some parents as well. For other parents, the roles were confining and demeaning for both men and women. Women were discouraged from careers outside the home and men were often stressed by the sole breadwinner role. Couples stayed together until the children were independent, which sometimes meant forever. Elkind (1994) notes those families' strong boundaries served the needs of the children more than the needs of the parents. Given today's diverse family forms, parental needs may be better served than those of children.

A new imbalance has been created with the loosening of roles and boundaries. Parents have greater relief from the confines of the earlier period, but children and adolescents experience greater stresses growing up with family rules, boundaries, and values that are ambiguous and ever-changing. Societal forces associated with the sexual revolution that has taken place during the past decades are changing and equalizing the roles and status of the sexes, thereby freeing up both men and women to assume roles and responsibilities once gender-associated. Couples, families, and children have had to change their living styles. As you assess the family, you must consider roles and role conflict as a cause of stress in individual and family functioning. You must also take into account the role of culture in determining and defining roles and responsibilities in the family. Each culture has different expectations and ideas concerning male-female roles and parent-child roles, and these must be reflected in your assessment.

Perhaps it is an oversimplification to attribute many of the problems children and their families experience to the changing family imbalance, but it does highlight what practitioners and social workers need to address in the assessment of family functioning. Assessment should focus on reducing family stressors and strengthening resources, which includes paying attention to reducing the stresses of both parents and children, not just the parents. This in turn enhances the resources of family members and the family as a social system. Examining the family member boundaries becomes a critical task of the practitioner in determining family interaction patterns, roles and power, and parenting issues. One of the first objectives in assessment is to identify the patterns of interaction among family members and the role and power assumed by individuals.

Also, the always stable and harmonious family is something of a myth (Allender et al., 1997; Elkind, 1994). Change and stress is experienced in all families throughout the developmental family life cycle. The developmental life cycle of families can be interrupted by divorce, separation, and remarriage, and all families—regardless of structure—experience multiple stressors as they move from one stage of family development to the next. Stressors are related to anxiety-provoking events as the family moves through time, coping with predictable family stages and events as well as unpredictable traumatic ones. The way families address this change and stress determines their level of adaptation or adjustment for continuing to perform family functions. How families handle stress will be affected by the family and will affect the family. Stress and coping is a "normal" occurrence in families, and new experiences and information from various systems can work to resolve many family issues. Practitioners will need to balance the family views, needs, and situation with the range of systems interacting with the family. Preventing compromises in development and strengthening competencies in individuals and the family system as a whole also is required. This is an example of system thinking illustrating the ecological or multisystemic perspective.

## Theoretical Basis for Family Assessment

Multisystemic family practice is influenced by the many ideas and values that are at the core of social work theory and practice. It is an integrative practice framework that encompasses basic social work values and serves to provide a critical appraisal of the various environments or social systems that surround children and families. Certain key assumptions and concepts are important to organizing information for assessments and for designing services.

### Key Assumptions

Family systems practice requires you to (1) build on the resources within the family and community, (2) focus attention on the family-environment interactions, and (3) recognize the effects of environmental factors on family and child functioning. Families are not homogeneous groups. Each perspective in a family will be unique. Begin with an examination of the family relationships and the dynamics of family circumstances. What happens between individuals in a family will influence family functioning and outcomes. Three influential components are (1) family relationship patterns, (2) family characteristics, and (3) sources of stress.

Families establish relationships, develop patterns, and create ways of organizing themselves that are unique to each family unit. Family patterns are seen in the quality of parent-child transactions, the experiences of families with their members, and the quality of health and safety provided by a family to its members. How a family goes about organizing itself and meeting the needs of its members is as important as who does it and what is accomplished in the process.

The quality of family relationships contributes to the social and emotional competence of children, which is central to their positive developmental outcomes and functioning (Huffman, Mehlinger, & Kerivan, 2000). Children's social and emotional competence will affect their later academic, behavioural, and social functioning. Parents and consistent caregivers play a protective role in developing social and emotional competence in children. Therefore, understanding the family relationship patterns and ways of interacting are very important in understanding the outcomes of both children and parents.

Family characteristics, such as the personal characteristics of parents, their family of origin experiences (historical events and current connections), and resources, such as competencies, social support, and material supports will affect the family's behavior patterns. Individuals and the extended family systems have a direct and indirect influence in how a family carries out its functions. Families are products of early experiences, learning, and current systemic influences. These can be both positive and negative influences and contribute to the development of resilience in families.

Stressors or demands on parental resources also positively or negatively influence the family's ability to function optimally. Stressors may be risk factors, which the family is unable to overcome, and therefore may lead to poor outcomes. When stressors are overcome, protective factors develop based on a positive experience and therefore, families develop resilience in coping with environmental stressors and demands. The strength of the multisystemic perspective is that it relies on assisting families in addressing their priorities in the context of their existing and potential relationships with available and accessible community resources and sources of support. As a result, focusing on family strengths encourages the development of family and individual resiliency and increases the opportunity for "good" outcomes.

The context for family practice is summarized as follows:

1. *Emotional Connections.* Families are bound by strong emotional ties, a sense of belonging, and a passion for being involved in one another's lives. Understanding family behavior and functioning in this context exerts a strong role in determining the nature of assistance a family needs to address its concerns, stressors, or situational difficulties. Changing the systems that interact with families changes families.

2. *Family as a Resource.* All families have strengths, often unappreciated or unrealized. Drawing on the family as a resource also makes full use of the family's inner resources. Understanding the complexity of the family envi-

ronment requires you to understand the uniqueness of families while understanding the intricacies of their situations. The family is the primary nurturing unit for individual well-being, and the source for the development of competence-resilience. Each family is unique. Families are not a homogeneous group.

3. *Family-Centered Approach.* Family-centered practices focus on relationships, interaction, and reciprocity. Information is learned about how family members impact and influence each other. The family determines changes in family members. Family members are the experts on their circumstances and experiences. Practitioner expertise assists families in managing the change process.

## Key Concepts

Understanding the significance of the environmental context of the family system is the key for assessing family process and outcomes. Focus on the family as a social system rather than on just the individual member systems in the family. Explore the ways the environments or systems interact to produce the dynamics within families and between families and their environments (Mattaini, 1999). In trying to explain why individuals act in the family as they do, practitioners know that the behavior of one member of a family is highly influenced by the behavior of other family members or the environments transacting with the family unit. In fact, all behaviors in a family are systematically influenced and related to one another. When one part of the system changes, this in turn produces change in other parts of that system. Interactions provide information.

Patterns of interacting are unique to each family system. Invisible boundaries delineate the family from other environments or systems, but allow for transactions from these systems (Minuchin, 1974). The family members interact with each other in ways that allow the best adaptation possible to a complex environment of family stress and conflict. Minuchin (1974) noted that families are often resistant to change while, at the same time, they are in a constant battle to achieve a balance.

Adaptation and flexibility are necessary for change. When the structure of the family system changes, the family is transformed, and family members are altered accordingly. Families adapt and change according to both internal and external conditions from the multiple systems impinging on them. As a result, each person's experiences change. When families are inflexible and unable to adapt, then maladaptive patterns emerge.

Five concepts are basic to understanding the family as a system:

1. The family as a system is greater than the sum of its individual systems.
2. The family system performs functions.
3. The family system develops system and subsystem boundaries.
4. The family system is ever evolving, creating a balance between change and stability.
5. Family behaviors are best understood from a circular causality rather than a linear causality.

These concepts are important to assessment and will provide meaningful information about the members of the family and how they are connected one to another.

---

**Concept 1**
The family as a system is greater than the sum of its individual systems.

---

This concept is especially useful in applications to practice because of two assumptions:

1. The parts are related to one another such that any change in one of the parts will have some effect on the others.
2. Each part is related to one or more of the other parts in a reasonably stable way during any particular period of time.

Recognizing that all behaviors in a family are systematically related to one another tells us that it is important that practitioners see all members of families to know how they work in order to understand the individual components or parts of that system. In other words, you will look beyond the individual in trying to explain the individual's behavior. You will understand the behavior, feelings, or functioning of a child or spouse if you understand the family as a whole. You do this by observing and hearing the interactions among family members, which is a richer context than just talking to individual family members. Who talks to whom? When does this occur? For example, if Martin, aged 10, is stealing from other children at school, you can try to understand the behavior simply in terms of Martin's motives, impulses, or other reasons. Or you can consider factors beyond the child and look at the larger context, his family, in an attempt to understand how the behavior is an expression of his family system. Then, if you can figure out how Martin's behavior is systematically related to the other parts of the family, you can change Martin's behavior by changing some aspects of the family's behavior, not just by changing the child. Martin's father may be ignoring him, except when he is in trouble, and Martin's mother may also be ignoring him and spending more time with his infant sister. Perhaps Martin's mother has been depressed since the birth of his sibling. You may learn that Martin's behavior changed only after the birth of his sibling. It is possible that Martin has few friends at school and his behavior is an attempt to be part of a friendship group. Martin, in order to get his father's attention and his mother's time, steals from other children at school. One way to stop the thefts would be to encourage the father and mother to find ways to spend more time with Martin, thus fulfilling his need.

Remember the large wooden Russian doll with many dolls inside it and each doll within the other one? Well, family systems are similarly embedded within other systems. It is useful to view the family as nested or "sitting" within parts of larger systems, such as the extended family, and even larger systems, such as the neighborhood, clan, or community, and work and social communities. Practitioners visualize this relationship between individuals, family, and their connections with others outside the family by drawing a set of circles called an ecomap. The circles outside the family can be depicted as larger or smaller, depending on the relationship of the family with these systems. When assessing families, it is initially very helpful to draw an ecomap. The ecomap is a graphic tool that helps us to look at the interacting factors that make up the total family environment. It gives us a picture or overview of the family in their situation and the environment of the family. It illustrates the "nested" or connected systems. Interfaces between the family and the community, its members, and others can be depicted in the ecomap. The strength of contacts with other systems is also shown graphically (see Chapter 4).

---

**Concept 2**
The family system performs functions.

---

A family has multiple purposes but essentially develops skills in its members for productive membership with other societal networks and participation in meaningful community life. Through its social network, the family processes information, makes decisions, engages in productive and expansive activities, and provides for individual growth and development. As a psychological environment the family provides its members with a sense of belonging and connectedness to each other. Attachment or emotional closeness develops and is integral to the survival of the unit and the development of social and emotional competence of individuals. Through its communication processes, the family shapes behavior, beliefs, and values of its members through acceptance and disapproval, attachment and bonding. This is accomplished through caring for and nurturing members yet assisting them to retain a separate identity from one another.

---

**Concept 3**
The family system develops system and subsystem boundaries.

---

Boundaries are invisible demarcations or dividers between family members or among parts of the system such as between parents and children or between the family and the community (Minuchin, 1974). Boundaries serve to define separateness and autonomy in a family and its subsystems. Examining and defining boundaries in families is very important. Boundaries can be created such as around belief systems, ideas, or roles. This suggests that some family members participate in some of the systems and not in others. Some members participate in multiple roles. Functions often define the boundaries, such as parent-child subsystems. Understanding normative family functions then makes it possible to construct boundaries or strengthen boundaries when necessary, as when disruption occurs because of lack of clarity in the distinctions between subsystems. Families will differ in how individuals are assigned to specific subsystems, or how easily individuals can move from one subsystem to anther.

Boundaries are permeable and regulate contact between systems. Boundaries exist between family members and these are described as rigid to diffuse depending on how open (permeable) or closed the boundary is. In general, the greater the clarity and distinction between boundaries in a family system, the more effective the family's functioning. When boundaries are too rigid, it discourages closeness among member and outside systems. Families with overly rigid boundaries are often referred to as disengaged families. This family system characteristic limits warmth, affection, and nurturing, but does foster independence. Families with diffuse boundaries are enmeshed with one another and offer mutual support but at the expense of independence and autonomy. Enmeshed families are loving and considerate but their members may have difficulty in their relationships with others outside the family (Nichols & Schwartz, 1998).

Most families have qualities of both boundary types at some point in time and under some circumstances. Understand, of course, that boundaries change across the life span. Healthy boundaries allow members to shift and change as needed. When working with families it is useful during assessment to consider the following questions about boundaries:

- Who is a member of this family system?
- What are the key systems involved with this family?
- What large systems does this family belong to?

Mapping techniques (see Chapter 4) called genograms and ecomaps provide a conceptual view of family systems and subsystems interacting with the family. These tools help practitioners and families to "see" the various systems and boundaries the family interacts with, such as spouse subsystem, parent-child subsystem, family-community subsystem. Constructing a visual model of the family's structure, interaction, and functioning helps both you and the family to have a complete picture of the family system and its social envirnment. From these visual tools practitioners can focus the inquiry or questions of assessment. Chapter 4 contains further discussion of these assessment tools.

Family structure is maintained by the boundary interactions of the family systems. There is a hierarchy of systems in families such as parent-child, marital, spousal, and sibling subsystems. These smaller units operate within the larger context of family. Each of these subsystems is organized to perform certain functions. Any number of subsystems can operate with a family, and any one individual may be a member of more than one subsystem. Boundaries operate between individuals or subsystems; they regulate the amount of contact that the individuals or subsystems have with each other (Nichols & Schwartz, 1998). Adaptive or effective family functioning is encouraged by clear boundaries, which allow for the encouragement of independence, but provide for an appropriate amount of affiliation (Nichols & Schwartz, 1998).

One of the important system functions that allows families to follow general rules is the innate power hierarchy within the family, which mandates that parents have more authority than children within the adaptive and well-functioning family (Minuchin, 1974). Family expectations emerge from the constant negotiation and interaction of subsystems. Consider the parenting subsystems, for example, in the Greene family. There are two adults: Mr. Greene and Mrs. Greene, a former husband and two children from Mrs. Greene's former marriage. In this family, the spousal subsystem is composed of Mr. and Mrs. Greene. The parent subsystem is organized to permit Mrs. Greene and her mother to fulfill the parenting functions. Mr. Greene and the children's father do not perform in this capacity. In assessing this arrangement, the important criterion is how effective this arrangement is in meeting the family's overall needs and the needs of the children. The Greenes may function very well in the described arrangement. One would expect such an arrangement to produce problems, however, if Mr. Greene and the children's biological father refused to accept the arrangements and interacted with the children in a way to produce conflict with Mrs. Greene and her mother. Similarly, problems could emerge if the new spouse, Mr. Greene, began to take on parenting functions and the mother-grandmother parenting subsystem failed to accept him in this role. This lack of clarity could be expected to produce problems until a new parenting arrangement was sorted out.

Families differ by their position along a continuum because the boundaries are too rigidly closed or are too easily crossed. Minuchin (1974) uses the terms *enmeshment* and *disengagement,* respectively, to refer to rigid or diffuse boundaries. Boundary problems occur when the family system rigidly adheres to one of these extremes. This is seen, for example, when parents in an enmeshed family may become tremendously upset because at dinner a child does not eat the dessert. On the other hand, the parents in a disengaged family may feel unconcerned about a child's dislike of school. The child may complain and show troubling behavior, but tensions likely will emerge in other parts of the family system and systems outside the family rather than between parents and child over the child's dislike of school.

Subsystems where boundaries are ill defined or too loose show comparable difficulties in families. Consider a family in which one or both parents have problems such a mental illness or alcoholism. In these situations one or more of the children often assume parenting functions when the parent is unavailable. Boundaries are assessed for their permeability and limiting factors. If boundaries are too permeable, the family identity and integrity is weak and the practitioner needs to strengthen the boundaries. If boundaries are too rigid, the family will need assistance to let new information and communication flow into it for optimal development and functioning. In each family, there will be unique boundaries, beliefs and expectations surrounding various subsystems, and role functioning and interactions with the larger systems. A great deal of family work centers on boundaries and boundary shifting.

---

**Concept 4**
The family system is ever-evolving, creating a balance between
change and stability.

---

Family systems are in a constant state of flux, shifting and changing with each interaction and achieving a balance within them. Change is both normal and necessary, but there is a tendency to perceive change as negative. Prolonged change in some families may lead to instability in the system. Temporary change may cause disruption briefly, as when a parent is hospitalised, but most family systems return to normal after such a disruption in a short period of time. When sustained change occurs in a family, there is a shift to a new balance, and then reorganization. An accident, a death, a birth, a job change, a reduced income, or illnesses are some events in the lives of families causing change and reorganization. While most families will reorganize ways to handle the changes, some families will not be able to adjust for lack of resources or other reasons and will need to find solutions outside the family. Practitioners help families find ways to obtain a balance and equilibrium, usually by identifying resources and solutions to their needs.

---

**Concept 5**
Family behaviors are best understood from a circular causality
rather than from a linear causality.

---

Parts of the family system interact to serve a particular function. The structure of these connections form patterns. Linear patterns are limited to sequences such as

$$A \longrightarrow B \longrightarrow C$$

In this example, A causes B, which results in C. Many events are linear in cause and effect, but not much information will be learned from linear interaction. When practitioners consider behavior and family communication from a circular perspective, information they learn will generally be more accurate. In family systems, circular patterns are formed and a closed recursive loop is the interaction pattern that is observed, as in the following diagram:

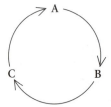

In this example, A and B interact to result in C, which in turn causes A—and a circular pattern emerges. The system is mutually reinforcing. The cyclic nature of these mutually reinforcing and influencing interactions can be positive or negative. When these interactions are negative, families find themselves locked into rigid patterns that can be very difficult to change without new interactions outside the family system. The timing and meaning give relevance to these patterns, and the relationships are reciprocal in nature (Tomm & Sanders, 1983).

Circularity is perhaps the most important concept in family interviewing. When practitioners ask questions of a linear nature, these are descriptive. Information gained from these questions is limited and only marginally helpful. An example of a linear question is this: Does dad worry about mom having another stroke? Questions producing much more, and more useful, information in family interviewing are circular questions. These questions produce information that is explored from a *difference* point of view. For example, What is the problem in the family now? What is the main concern about mom now? What problem does this pose for the children? How is this different from before? Who agrees with you about this problem? What does her behavior mean to you?

By exploring differences among the family members, practitioners can identify the specific behaviors perceived to be problematic. *Explore differences between perceptions, objects, events, meanings, and ideas* (Franklin & Jordan, 1999). Each member of the family mutually contributes to the adaptive and maladaptive family interaction. Each person's behavior influences that of the other. The perception of each family member is valued and important in helping families construct a new way of viewing each other so they can break out of their maladaptive cycle. Families, who rarely understand the cycles of their interaction, need assistance to move from the linear to the circular perspective of causation. Table 3.1 shows examples of circular questions for general situations.

**Table 3.1** Examples of Circular Questions

| Exploring Present Situation | Exploring Past Situation | Exploring Future or Hypothetical Situation |
|---|---|---|
| Who does what when? | Who did what then? | What would she do differently if he did (not) do this? |
| Then what happens? | What solutions were tried? | |
| What next? | | |
| Where is she when this happens? | | |
| What does she do? | | |
| Then what do they do? | | |
| Who notices first? | | |
| What does he respond? | | |
| When he does not do that, what happens? | | |
| **Exploring Difference** | **Exploring Difference** | **Exploring Difference** |
| Has it always been this way? | How was it different? | How would it be different if she were to do this? |
| | When was it different? | |
| | What else was different then? | |
| | How does that differ from how it is now? | |
| | Was it then more or less than it is now? | |
| **Agreement/Disagreement** | **Agreement/Disagreement** | **Agreement/Disagreement** |
| Who agrees with you that this is how it happens? | Who agrees with you? | Who would agree with you this is probably what would happen? |
| **Explanation/Meaning** | **Explanation/Meaning** | **Explanation/Meaning** |
| What is your explanation for this? | How do you explain this change? | Tell me why you believe this would happen? |
| What does this mean to you? | What does this change (or lack of change) mean to you? | How do you think your wife would explain it? |
| | | What would this mean to you? |

*Source:* Adapted from "The Evolution of Circular Questions: Training Family Therapists," by C. Fleuridas, T. S. Nelson, and D. M. Rosenthal, 1986, *Journal of Marital and Family Therapy, 12,* Table 3, pp. 120–125, American Association for Marriage and Family Therapy.

Helping families to change is not an easy task. Family members' vision of possible outcomes may not always be consistent, and trying to identify a common and shared outcome among members is important to this process. Describing concerns is easy, but finding a shared vision requires the practitioner to help the family understand how the current situation differs from the desired goal-state, and to clarify the necessary steps to move from one to the other (Mattaini, 1999).

## Family Development

Theory and concepts of family development contribute to an understanding of family functioning by considering developmental issues, stress, coping and adaptations, and cognitive development. Families, in general, move through certain stages and perform a number of tasks and key processes. The literature identifies different stages emerging for single-parent, divorced or remarried, adoptive, and other family structures. While it is not necessarily meant to portray all families, the mainstream family development framework (Carter & McGoldrick, 1988; Wright & Leahey, 1994) is a useful way to look at what is happening in a family. Determine the stage the family is experiencing and the tasks associated with that stage; then decide whether the attachments emerging are adaptive or maladaptive.

*Stages.* The following developmental stages are presented as a guide only and may not be relevant for every family. The developmental stages and transitions of families are these:

- *Single young adult.* Launching of single young adult—differentiate self from family of origin.
- *Couple stage.* Marriage and joining of families—establish a couple identity through negotiating issues, rules, and traditions.
- *Childbearing and preschool children stage.* Introduction of children into the family. The couple joins in child rearing, financial, and household tasks. Realign relationships with extended family to include parenting and grandparenting roles.
- *School-age children.* Period when children are in school—kindergarten through high school.
- *Families with adolescents.* Shifting in parent-child relationships to permit adolescents to move in and out of the system. Begin shift toward joint caring for elders.
- *Launching children.* Renegotiate marital system as a dyad. Develop adult-to-adult relationships with grown children and parents.
- *Parents in middle age.* Maintaining own or couple functioning and beginning interest in physiological decline. Deal with loss of spouse, siblings, and peers.
- *Aging parents.* Generally dealing with a slower life pace. Almost all retired, and many adjusting to some physiological slowing. But aging parental roles are changing as adults live longer and have new opportunities to pursue.

*Tasks.* As an ever-changing system, families master the tasks and stresses associated with each phase, developing resilience, strengths, and competencies. When tasks are not successfully carried out or are impeded, difficulties can occur creating stressors and disruptions. For example, parents may have fears about an adolescent moving out of the home to college. Conflicts may arise between the adolescent and parents and the parents may prevent the young adult from leaving home, seeking freedom, and self-direction. This may delay the young adult's development.

A crisis can impact family development. The unexpected birth of a child to one of the adolescent children in the family is an example. A crisis can be overcome, or it can be so traumatic that the family never returns to its former competent level of functioning. Events can impact the family structure and family membership and tasks at every stage.

*Attachments.* Each family will be unique in terms of the relational processes they experience. Relationship patterns in the family system expand and contract at various stages, realigning over the life span as members come and go and move on through their personal development. Exploring family connections or attachments helps the practitioner understand the quality of interpersonal relationships within the family. The type or quality of emotional attachments established with family members is likely to determine the kinds of relationships established later in life with others, including spouses and children (DeMaria, Weeks, & Hof, 1999; Minuchin, 1974). The quality of family relational experiences provides a base for understanding family functioning, especially patterns of closeness and distance.

## Family Structure

One common family form is the single-parent family. This family structure is prevalent today and typically is formed by either a never-married mother or a divorced one. Father-led households are less common, and the major distinguishing feature between the two households is the disparity in household income. Young, never-married mothers with young children are among the poorest families today. Increasingly, there are single persons, male or female, gay or straight, who are adopting children to form families. Such families are still small in numbers, but they certainly face considerable stressors from the environment.

Remarried or blended families are one of the most common forms of changing family structure. Reconstituted families will go through restructuring of family boundaries as they address issues of parenting, power, and intergenerational concerns. Multiple internal and external stressors often accompany these family forms as parents work through agreements for the new family group. For an in-depth discussion of the life cycle stages, see Carter and McGoldrick (1988) and Goldenberg and Goldenberg (2000).

## Family Culture

Culture impacts a family's structural, developmental, and functional aspects. Culture refers to the distinct way the family behaves, thinks, and communicates, permeating its customs, beliefs, and values (Cross, Bazron, Dennis, & Isaacs, 1989).

Practitioners need to have self-awareness of their own cultural orientation and its impact on families. In their interactions with families, there will be dynamics that practitioners must acknowledge, adjust to, and accept. This self-awareness will be helpful as practitioners work with the family's natural and informal supports and helping networks within the community of the family. Included among these are neighborhoods, schools, churches, and other institutions.

Emphasis should be on the strengths inherent in all cultures and ways to use these strengths for the unique needs, treatment issues, and concerns of families. The focus should not be on advocating alternative family remedies, but rather on working with families and their circumstances, valuing diversity and respecting its worth. The implications for practice are that families' differences are as important as their similarities. All families share common basic needs, but there are differences in how families of various cultures meet those needs. Each culture finds some behaviors, interactions, or values more important or desirable than others, and knowing this can help you interact more successfully with differing cultures. Awareness and acceptance of differences in communication, life view, and definitions of health and family are critical to the successful delivery of interventions (Cross, Bazron, Dennis, & Isaacs, 1989).

These guiding principles can help as you work with families of various cultures:

1. Respect the unique, culturally defined needs of various populations.
2. Acknowledge the role that culture plays in shaping behaviors, values, and views of society.
3. Recognize primary sources of support for minority populations that are natural helping systems, such as churches, community leaders, extended family members, healers, and others.
4. Acknowledge differences in the concept of "family" and "community" among various cultures and even subgroups within cultures.
5. Remember that minority populations are usually best served by persons who are part of that culture.
6. When working with minority families, know that process is as important as outcome. Recognize that taking the best of both worlds enhances the capacity of both family and practitioner.
7. Understand and recognize when values of minority families are in conflict with dominant society values.
8. Practice with the knowledge that some behaviors are adjustments to being different (Cross, Bazron, Dennis, & Isaacs, 1989; Okun, 1996).

Acknowledging cultural differences and being aware of how they affect the helping process is the starting point for discussion with culturally different families. You may need to adapt your assessment approaches because the dynamics of difference can be most problematic at this stage (McGill, 1992). For example, Latino children may have caretakers whom they refer to as "mom" and "dad" but who may not legally be guardians. Indian mothers may leave younger children in the care of older children as a commonly accepted practice in their communities. In black families, a man may not be an "official" part of the household but may be an integral part of the family system. Furthermore, time concepts may be different, and formal appointment times may not be accepted or understood. Work hours, spiritual practices, or family obligations may conflict with traditional practices of agencies and organizations for home visit appointments. Each of these situations could be interpreted as weakness or family maladaption if the practitioner is not sensitive to cultural behaviors of the family. Determining what is normative in the context of the family's culture is necessary for obtaining accurate assessment information.

The use of evaluation measures needs to be carefully considered, as tools may be biased by misinterpretations of language. The key to successful assessment and intervention is the ability to communicate respect and separate the cultural factors from social economic factors (McGill, 1992). In an effort to simplify the complexity of working in a multicultural context, McGill (1992) and DeMaria, Weeks, and Hof (1999) suggest the following questions to ask families for cultural information as a way to understand needs and concerns:

Where did the family come from?

When did they come to this country?

What were the circumstances that brought them to this country?

What is important to this family?

Who are the current members of this family?

What kind of people would they describe themselves as?

How do family members describe themselves racially?

How do you define yourself?

What good and bad things have happened to them over time?

What were or are the group's experiences with oppression?

What lessons have they learned from their experiences?

What are the ways in which pride and shame issues are shown in this family?

These questions examine the family experiences both within the family and through the members' larger group/community experiences and biases. Knowledge and understanding of the family's collective story of how they have been coping with life events and how they have responded to pain and troubles can emerge. The practitioner hears the context of the family concerns within the current context and then meaning becomes clearer. Furthermore, genograms and ecomaps (see Chapter 4) can offer a graphic way to capture the unit's cultural story while encouraging a systematic view of the family and its functioning. The use of the genogram determines the family structure by generation and kin relationships in a culturally sensitive context.

## Family Beliefs

Family beliefs are the attitudes and expectations that influence various areas of family functioning. Identifying and clarifying the beliefs held in families helps families and practitioners understand the interactions and alliances formed in families. It explains family behaviors and informs us about family functioning. Beliefs and assumptions develop from family experiences and are intricately connected to behavior.

Over time, family members may have learned rules and beliefs that are not necessarily accurate, and these may have led to the development of myths. A family myth is a false belief that justifies and sustains ongoing patterns of interaction, patterns that are generally not positive (Wright & Leahey, 1984, p. 63). Family exchanges are shaped by these unwritten rules or beliefs about events and situations. Helping family members articulate the beliefs and examine them is an important intervention. For example, a belief may be that family members cannot disagree with mother because she may become depressed again and end up in the hospital. Therefore, family members remain silent and apprehensive about discussing their differences of opinion. The result of the silence is that tension builds and family members feel that "they walk around on eggs" trying not to upset mother. The children resent mother's unstable health, and father is angry for having to speak for the children. In this example, the practitioner must articulate the rules and then check out the beliefs with each family member, asking, What happens when people in this family disagree with mother? What would happen to mother if you expressed your thoughts and feelings? Identifying beliefs can increase or decrease solution options when problems arise. Different views need to be tolerated in families. How families adapt to various stressors depends on the beliefs they hold, and in the same way, the beliefs of the practitioner about the family and their stressors profoundly affect how the family is approached by, engaged by, and receives services from the practitioner.

## Family Rituals and Traditions

Rituals are effective on a number of levels. They involve action, cognitive understanding and reflection, and insight. Rituals provide a way of controlling the often overwhelming emotion that is typically associated with a crisis and give clear expectations for action at a time when problem-solving abilities are limited. Rituals also offer a connection to intergenerational culture both societal and interfamilial. And they are appealing, because many families have lost the rituals that formerly guided their behavior and beliefs, often because they have lost their connection to former generations. Transitions, such as parenthood, divorce, adolescence, reunions, and graduations, may need to be marked by rituals. Rituals prescribe behavior, hierarchies, and boundaries.

Rituals and traditions can block individuals in healthy development and reinforce the need for rebellion in response to rigidity, but they can also draw the family together in an opportunity to celebrate events. Families can be understood in the rituals and traditions that arise from their religion, culture, and racial identity. How are important times, events, and situations recognized and celebrated? Meaning is attached to these events for a family through special foods, family humor, and getting together and celebrating.

Families who make opportunities to join together in traditions have a sense of commitment and emotional bonding. When this is lacking, a practitioner's intervention may be needed to help a family create a ritual or tradition for enhancing family commitments, loyalties, and sense of connections. The ritual calls the family to join in new combinations or alliances not then found in the family system. Various levels of importance with family systems are tied to beliefs, roles, rituals, and traditions, such as Christmas, Hanukkah, and Ramadan. Here is an example of ritual in therapy from Sargeant (1985):

The husband of a married couple had an extramarital affair. In order to move forward with the wife, who found it difficult to forgive the husband, the practitioner designed a ritual. The couple needed to leave the "old marriage" and start a "new marriage." The couple referred to their need to bury the old and to begin anew. The practitioner noted the lack of transition between the old and the new and presented the ritual as that transition. The ritual included acknowledging both the good and the dysfunctional aspect of the old relationship. For this couple, the ritual provided a way of leaving the "old" marriage behind and beginning to focus energies on rebuilding a more workable relationship. This is significant as frequently with this type of presenting concern, couples become stuck on the ability of one spouse to forgive the other, rather than on the ability and commitment to rebuilding. It is important to note that this provides one point of redirection but is not the sum total of the work the couple invests in.

For rituals and traditions to have family meaning and significance they must be repeated and must be "coordinated in order to provide a sense of predictability, connections, and a way to enact values" (Doherty, cited in DeMaria, Weeks, & Hof, 1999, p. 183).

Questions to ask families about rituals and traditions include these:

- How does this family celebrate rituals of *connection*? Family meals, bedtimes, daily leaving and coming home, holidays, weekday rituals, couple rituals, child rituals
- How does this family *observe* these rituals of celebration? Birthdays, school success, holidays, religious passage, births, marriages, and other meaningful passages (DeMaria, Weeks, & Hof, 1999, p. 183)

Rituals and traditions may influence roles within the family; therefore, it is important to conceptualize rituals from a family perspective rather than from the viewpoint of the individual. Rituals are used to break rigidity and to reinforce boundaries of a family system.

## Family Functioning

Families function on many different levels and have needs ranging from basic to complex, covering the spectrum from physical needs, such as food and shelter, to self-actualization. Assessment examines the way a family fulfills certain common needs by asking about roles, tasks, and responsibilities. Determining whether basic functions of minimal safety, stability, and nurturing occur in the family is the first step. Once basic functioning is understood, the practitioner determines the adequacy of boundaries—parenting and authority. Do the parents set and maintain limits for the family members? Are the limits sufficient for the situation? If not, is stability of the whole family system threatened? A summary of family functioning and tasks, and the interventions that can be helpful are presented in Table 3.2: Basic Family Functioning Needs and Resources (Kilpatrick & Holland, 1995, p. 6). Common issues often center on the needs identified in the table.

A basic family function is to provide food, shelter, safety or protection, health and nurturance for its members. A family that is functioning well will provide the following:

- *Stability and safety for the child and family.* Families must provide a continuous caring and nurturing environment necessary for children if these children are to develop family identity and a sense of belonging where attachments are formed. Children must feel and be safe in the family environment. Stability is also related to providing financial security. Families must have adequate financial resources to secure food and shelter on a continuous basis.

- *Heath and education.* Families safeguard health and provide nutrition for healthy growth and learning. Families also teach morality, respect, public acceptability, self-care, socialization, and social roles.

- *Competence.* Families provide emotional support so that social emotional competence of its members can emerge. The family is also a source of self-esteem, motivation for achievement, and work orientation for its members; it gives them religious and spiritual orientation, family ties, and values.

Family functioning reflects the rigidity and maintenance of boundaries, relational patterns, the family of origin experience, and the current context—including cultural and value orientations of the family. Table 3.2 offers guidelines to practitioners in assessing family functioning issues and determining the interventions that can address these.

In addition, adaptive family functioning includes good communication among family members and low levels of family conflict (Green & Werner, 1996). An important component of good communication is the degree to which family members are open, honest, self-revealing, and direct with each other. How open families are in expressing feelings, including anger and conflict, indicates their degree of expressiveness. Families with a full range of expression of feelings—from happiness to sadness to anger—are healthy. Families with rigid patterns of emotional expression within a narrow range are considered to be unhealthy. Verbal and nonverbal ways of family communication patterns are relevant to assessment.

Family functioning is also influenced by power and control in the family system. Power and control are exhibited in various ways. Instrumental means include the use of objects or privileges—for example, access to television, toys, and movies. Psychological power and control refer to communication and feelings used to influence behaviors, such as praise, criticism, and imposition of guilt. Corporal control includes physical punishment, hugging, and spanking. Positive and negative control and influence operate in all families, and examining the rules, how they are enforced, and by whom, establishes the appropriateness and consistency with which power and control are used in the family (Wright & Leahey, 1984).

**Table 3.2** Basic Family Functioning Needs and Resources

| Functioning | Family Tasks | Intervention Strategy | Intervention Technique |
|---|---|---|---|
| **Level 1** | | | |
| Physical & Life Sustaining: food, shelter, protection, medical care, and nurturance | Having the ability to carry out and manage all nurturing needs, and provide food, shelter, safety, and medical care | Focus on Strengths:<br>• Focus on family strengths, not problems<br>• Obtain support to enhance family capacity to meet basic Level 1 needs | Focus on Family/Community Resources:<br>• Family preservation<br>• Case management<br>• Support network<br>• Parent teaching strategies |
| **Level 2** | | | |
| Limits and safety | Having sufficient authority to provide minimal structure, limits, and safety | Focus on Strengths:<br>• Strengthen the parental/caretaking role<br>• Reestablish authority with those in need of control<br>• Increase clarity of expectations | Focus on Parent/Couple, Family/Community:<br>• Parental coalitions<br>• Well-defined limits<br>• Clear communication<br>• Social learning skills<br>• Behavior contracts and reinforcers<br>• Task assignments |
| **Level 3** | | | |
| Clear, appropriate boundaries at family, individual, and generational levels | Ensuring maintenance of space and boundaries | Focus on Boundaries:<br>• Focus on problems<br>• Clarify the ideal family structure, considering the ethnic and family expectations<br>• Increase generational clarity | Focus on Couple and Individual:<br>• Protect family, individual, and generational boundaries<br>• Rebuild alliances<br>• Balance triangles<br>• Make task assignments<br>• Strengthen communication skills |
| **Level 4** | | | |
| Inner conflict intimacy, self-actualization, insight | Addressing issues of inner conflict, self-actualization of family members | Focus on Problems:<br>• Clarify and resolve earlier trauma; gain understanding | Focus on Individual:<br>• Narrative interventions<br>• Intergenerational issues<br>• Family sculpture |

*Source: Adapted from Allie C. Kilpatrick and Thomas P. Holland,* Working with Families, *pp. 5–6. Copyright © 1995 Allyn & Bacon. Adapted by permission.*

Finally, alliances, coalitions, or triangles also describe family relationships. These family patterns may be healthy coalitions or they can be problematic. Some examples of power, control, and alliances are these:

- A complementary alliance—e.g., mother and child subsystem: unequal.
- Symmetrical alliance—e.g., between spouses: equal.
- Triangle—a third person brought in to diffuse high anxiety within a dyad. This dilutes high emotionality and anxiety.
- Multimember coalitions—alignment of two or more members against a third.
- Attachments—strong emotional bonds between members.

Determining these connections and relationships in family systems is important to understanding their current functioning.

A family can be very skillful and powerful at drawing an outsider into its point of view. By using systems theory and concepts about family change, the practitioners can minimize this danger, knowing what to look for in terms of information—and where to look for the information—while remaining relatively unaffected by the family dynamics. Not all information will fit the practice framework and there is always a risk of ignoring important data. Nevertheless, to understand individual behavior within the context of family, and the multiple systems transacting with it, you will use the most relevant framework to make sense of what you are seeing and hearing.

## *Summary of Key Practice Principles*

1. The framework for family practice is directed by thinking "family as context," informed by belief systems wherein the family is a special social environment conceptualized as consisting of multiple systems.

2. Each system is interactive and interdependent with parts of itself and with other systems it relates to. People, or groups of people, and the multiple systems interacting with them, mutually influence each other's behavior.

3. A family is more than the sum of its individual parts. It is a unique system with particular responsibilities and functions. It is purposeful and receives input from the components or members of that system, as well as from the environment outside the system.

4. A change affects all family members. The family is able or unable to create a balance between change and stability.

5. Systems theory is complex and difficult to apply to real-life family situations. It does help us understand families and their social environments, and how to locate the place for intervention. It does not tell us which interventions to use but evidence-supported practice assists with that decision (Fraser, 1997; Williams & Ell, 1998).

6. By approaching a complicated family situation from a systems theory perspective, using this as the foundation for understanding the family, the practitioner is able to be somewhat more objective about the family issues.

7. Utilizing a multiple systemic perspective for family assessment and intervention addresses many important aspects in helping families and the systems interacting and supporting the individuals in families.

8. Individual members' behavior has an effect on and influences other family members. Family members' behaviors are best understood as having a circular rather than a linear causality. Although not discussed here, feminist family therapists emphatically object to the notion of circular causality because it leads to blaming the victim as much as the perpetrator in families where there is violence and maltreatment (Goldner, Penn, Sheinberg, & Walker, 1990).

9. Practitioners who see the family context as interactions of multiple systems—the family and its social environments—will be better able to build on strengths in families and promote family self-change, a notion critical to practice.

## Learning Activities

### Activity 3.1: Tracing Family Development

*Instructions:* This activity can be done individually and as a group. If used as a group activity, individuals work in small groups first, and then share their family development as a group. Look for similarities and differences or uniqueness among families and their development.

Some family events are normal and occur for everyone, such as starting kindergarten, starting school, marriage, and dating. Other events are specific to a family and can dramatically change the life course for a family—for example, death, divorce, loss of home, a move, inheritance, and so on.

- Identify six normative historical family events in your family. How did these events impact individuals in the family and the family as a system?
- Identify six unique historical family events. How did these events impact individuals in the family and the family as a system?

Share these events with colleagues or your group.

### Activity 3.2: My Family Journal

1. What messages did you receive from family members about the importance or role of children?

2. Identify two rituals of connection in your family, and then describe how these traditions were celebrated in the family. Do you still observe these rituals and traditions?
   (a) Ritual:
       How Observed?
   (b) Ritual:
       How Observed?

*Activity 3.3: Case Study*

Read the Del Sol family case study (see Chapter 9) and complete the following based on the case information.

1. Describe the cultural affiliations that exist in the family.
2. Based on the cultural affiliations of this family, describe how you would approach assessment.
3. Give an example of cultural beliefs and how these influence self-esteem, marriage, parenting, sexuality, familial responsibility, and loyalties.
4. Design a ritual for this family to address a need.

---

▼▼▼

# CHAPTER FOUR

# Family Assessment

F amily assessment is a process of collecting data about a family's functioning. It begins with the first contact. Data are collected from the family interview about family strengths and problems, concerns are prioritized, and a decision is made about intervention. Assessment should provide a profile of a family's unique strengths, needs, and goals that result in "tailored" interventions for change. Assessment interviews have several aims and outcomes: (1) to determine the family system functioning, (2) to assess family strengths, (3) to determine areas for change, and (4) to make appropriate recommendations for intervention.

Change is sought in individual and family functioning in the areas of family patterns (boundaries) and family functioning (roles, tasks, and communications) and often with interactions the family has with the community environment. The degree of change sought will depend on the family's needs and goals and on the skill of the practitioner. It may be as simple as behavior change or as complex as a change in the whole family system. Preparing to interview a family requires reflection on the family as a system and knowledge of family issues prior to the first interview. Remember that not all presenting concerns require resolution.

## Preparation for the Assessment

All family members should be invited to the first interview, and for a complete assessment, all should be present. Emphasizing that everyone should attend is a powerful restructuring and reframing move, indicating that the whole family is involved in the problem (Nichols & Schwartz, 1998) and that a family meeting is often the first step in initiating change. Some practitioners feel so strongly about this that they refuse to see families if all members do not come to the meetings. However, it is advisable to see those who come and to encourage the missing members to participate. The disadvantage of a missing member is that you do not have that person's perspective. If key family members fail to participate in the first meeting, their absence is indicative of a family structural problem (boundaries).

A decision to work with various subsystems may emerge after the initial meeting or if the practitioner believes there is good reason to do so, such as seeing the marital couple without children to discuss matters of their sexual relationship. Even while working with smaller units, however (spouse subsystem, parent-child subsystem), the practitioner keeps a focus on family issues (Hepworth, Rooney, & Larsen, 1997; Franklin, & Jordan, 1992). For most family issues, the whole family system is seen together. Sometimes others in the household are invited, such as grandparents.

Having identified the context of the family issues and the strengths of the family through the first interview, the practitioner may decide not to invite all the members to the following interview. If this is the case, you must maintain the family system perspective throughout for the eventual return to family interviews. Successful joining with the family system is required for good family interviews. The terms *joining* and *accommodation* are used to describe how the practitioner attempts to put the family at ease and adjusts to accept their organization and style (Nichols & Schwartz, 1998).

## *Assessment Approaches*

Assessment approaches and the types of tools employed during the meeting vary depending where one looks for problems and what one sees. For example, looking at the whole family, looking at dyads or individuals, or focusing on the problems that maintain symptoms will determine the activities. For the first contact, interviews are generally the most accepted approach; structured evaluation procedures can be introduced later (Nichols & Schwartz, 1998). Whatever data-gathering method is used, a thorough assessment of the family structure is the initial step.

Although interviews are the most common method for collecting data, they have one major drawback: they are the least systematic way to obtain information. Other assessment approaches, which involve formal tools and instruments, may be more efficient for collecting and organizing information, but they may seem less personal to the family at the first meeting. Practitioners need to select a method with which they and the family are comfortable.

In general, practitioners will use either direct or indirect approaches in the data-gathering process. Direct approaches involve interviews, using both standardized and nonstandardized formats; mapping and graphic methods; and behavioral observations through experiential and task assignments that allow the practitioner to observe family interaction firsthand. Indirect approaches provide information from background information sheets, treatment or service records, questionnaires, self-report scales and measures, family goals, journals, and diaries (Jordan & Franklin, 1995). All assessment methods have strengths and limitations. Some require considerable competence in their use; some will provide greater accuracy than others. No method is adequate for all situations. One of the skills a practitioner will develop is learning which method is best in which circumstance.

Many family and parent-child problems are best examined through a combination of assessment approaches—using interviews supported with standardized measures. As a form of decision making, practitioners and organizations use interviews with the greatest frequency to obtain family assessment information. Standardized approaches to the assessment of problems in families provide data of greater accuracy because these assessment tools are grounded in research. Standardized assessment measures give us information by formulating a score about an issue, feeling, perception, and attitude or severity of a problem. Combining information collected in interviews with data from standardized measures produces more reliable family information than data collected with a single method. Assessment measures ideally will be tools that are (a) reliable and valid, (b) easy to use, (c) easy to interpret, and (d) culturally sensitive and free of gender bias.

## Tools for Collecting and Organizing Data

Four types of tools for collecting data are discussed in this section:(1) the family interview, (2) mapping and graphic tools, (3) self-report tools, and (4) teaching and role-play tools. Although each method of data collection can be used alone, family interviews with the addition of other tools probably provide the best source of information for a practitioner to become aware of the family's dynamics and events that make up their life. The use of tools is also the best way to monitor change.

Finding ways to organize interview data is a challenge for the beginning practitioner. Family assessment requires you to know the internal and external factors that impact the family, and a number of basic tools can assist you beyond the interview to focus on what changes will maximize and support the family resources while providing more adequate family organization. Tools that can help organize data from or during interviews are the genogram, ecomap, and social network map and grid. Each is simple to use and requires pencil and paper, a blackboard and chalk, or a flip chart and marker. Observational and teaching tools can help you provide interventions for families while teaching a behavior, labeling a feeling, coaching, or shaping behavior for improved communication and change in family alliances and coalitions.

## The Family Interview

There are numerous good books and courses on interviewing and it is not the intent here to teach the reader how to interview, but to review basic guidelines. First, the basic interview guidelines are presented followed by an overview of the process of the interview.

*Preparing for a Family Interview*  Underlying all successful interviews is the ability to communicate clearly and the ability to understand the communications of the family members. A family interview is affected by several elements:

- practitioner and family characteristics, such as physical, cognitive, and affective factors
- message components: language, nonverbal cues, and sensory cues
- interview climate: physical, social, temporal, and psychological factors

Your task is to control for as many of these factors as possible in order to obtain as much information as possible about family and member concerns. However, you cannot control them all; therefore, you must consider how these factors contribute to and interweave within the interview process, and affect your judgment about the information obtained. Some of the factors that influence the interview (Sattler, 1998) are listed below:

### Environmental factors—*be aware of the surroundings.*

- Interview the family in their home to see how they interact with the environment, or when this is not possible, hold the family meeting in a private, quiet, comfortable sized room in the office with no disturbances.
- *Never* interview a child or victim of violence while the alleged offender is in the room or in the building.
- Conduct the interview in a safe and friendly environment and allot as much time as needed.

### Listening—*listening skills lead to informed impressions.*

- Do not become preoccupied with what you are going to say next or what questions to ask. This is distracting and you will miss what the person is saying and how he or she is saying it.
- The ebb and flow of the interaction will continually modify the impressions both of you have.
- Impressions emerge throughout, but do not allow them to bias your interview until you have a complete picture of all family information or without testing your initial hypotheses of the family problems.

### Listening to yourself—*learn about yourself from everything you do.*

- Become attuned to your thoughts, feelings, and actions, and learn how to deal with them appropriately during the family interview.
- Especially for beginning practitioners, and whenever possible, the family interviews should be videotaped, or conducted under live supervision through a one-way mirror. This is an excellent method to see how your needs, values, belief system, and standards and skills emerged during the interview and how this may have affected the family and their responses.

### Body language—*body language conveys meaning.*

- Be aware of your body language and what you do when talking or listening. You may unknowingly bite your nails, crack your knuckles, twirl your hair, tap your pen, rock in your chair, play with your hands, move your foot, or display any other nervous habit that may distract or annoy family members in the interview.

- Supportive and accepting body language will put everyone at ease and convey a message of empathy and trust that allows the family to express themselves.
- Be cognizant of your body language and what it may convey to persons of different backgrounds as you conduct the interview. You may have to alter your stance, posture, eye contact, or place of chair, depending on what background or culture the family celebrates.

**Observing family language and behavior—***observe the words and behaviors of each family member throughout.*

- Notice if there are any differences in how the child behaves when he or she is with or without certain family members.
- Pay attention to facial expression, postures, vocal behaviors, mannerisms, gestures, and motor behavior of each member. Videotaping the interview is helpful because practitioner and family behavior and subtle nuances may not be detected when you are first learning about family dynamics, and they may prove to be invaluable to the successful outcome of family change.
- Pay attention to the logic of the communication. It is important to hear not just the words but the inflection, tone, and speed of the communication.

Of course, practicing interviews helps you improve, and good supervision is essential.

*Planning for the First Interview*    Planning for the first interview before the family meeting is critical. Some guidelines include the following:

1. The first interview is a planned event with the whole family. Book an appointment inviting the whole family to the meeting.
2. A family interview can take place anywhere—in the family home, in an office, in a room in a school, or other place convenient for all. Advantages to the home visit include the possibility of seeing the complete family—infants, grandparents, the boarder, and any others who form part of the family's social environment. Seeing the home gives you an opportunity to see firsthand the physical environment and other interactions, which may not occur naturally in the office settings—for example, how parental competencies are carried out, the patterns of coming and going, and other social and interactional patterns that may be constrained in the office setting. Cultural and ethnic uniqueness can be observed more deeply in the home. Sleeping, cooking, and home management may be noted, as well as any other aspects that may contribute to family stressors.

   Seeing the family in the work setting does offer some advantages to the practitioner. There is more privacy than in the family home, and control of the interview is possible without interruptions. Consultation and even live supervision may be available. However, many families find the office setting intimidating and inconvenient to reach. Some settings may reinforce the idea that one member is ill—for example, interviewing in the psychiatric setting may inadvertently foster the belief that mom is the sick one, an individual-based concern, and this belief may create difficulty in focusing on the family unit and the need for change in the whole family.

3. The purpose of the first interview is to obtain a broad picture of information about who the family is and the concerns, issues, and sources of stress. Various settings will require that you focus and collect information specific to the services. For example, a child and adolescent service will focus on the parent and parent-child issues, while a hospital asthma clinic may require you to focus more on the health aspects of the person with asthma, including a specific medical history.

4. Prior to meeting with the family, consider the purpose of the meeting: Are you trying to determine how well a family is coping with a member who has cancer, or are you assessing for family violence? The purpose determines how the meeting is conducted and the flow of questions may be different.

5. Family therapists (Tomm, 1984) suggest also that planning begins by designing hypotheses of the family relational patterns. There are no right or wrong explanations of what is happening. Hunches emerge that need to be tested. The hypotheses are designed to provide general direction for exploring the family's situation and to generate the most helpful explanations of the family's behavior—how a family is functioning. These hypotheses will guide the interview questions.

6. Invite the whole family to the interview at a designated time.

7. At the beginning of the interview set the foundation for participation and work by establishing the rules of operating. Ask parents to handle the children in whatever way they usually do in the case of young children. Explain that participants will be expected to contribute. Make everyone feel comfortable. Minimize chaos and make the environment welcoming. This is necessary for joining the family.

8. There are four stages to family interviews—engagement, assessment, intervention, and termination. Every interview follows these stages and the process follows these stages over the course of your contact with the family

    *Engagement.* Establish and maintain a relational contact for therapeutic work to occur. Active listening, empathy, warmth, and respect are important qualities to demonstrate with everyone. Practitioners must not show alliances with any one family member (Tomm, 1984).

    *Assessment.* Establish the concerns of the family. Here the focus is on identifying family resources, relationships between family members and problems, issues, and concerns. Determine the attempted solutions and explore what changes the family wants. This may take place over several family meetings. Do not engage in confrontation or interpretation of information too quickly, since this may impede progress.

    *Intervention.* This provides the context for change. Family therapists (Tomm, 1984) emphasize the need for assignments, tasks, and rituals and traditions (repeated patterns) to effect change. Beginning practitioners may need consultation with this task. Intervention can occur over three sessions and be effective according to Epstein and Bishop (1981) of the McMaster

Model of Family Functioning, Gurman and Kniskern (1981), and Thomlison (1984). Brief or short-term interventions are as effective as long-term treatment. Change will occur in the individual system, the marital system, and the family as a whole.

*Termination.* The family finishes with the practitioner and is encouraged to contact the practitioner if future concerns arise.

Table 4.1, Questions for the First Family Interview, provides samples of the types of questions that should be asked in the first meeting with a family. Other topics to consider are the circular questions and family functioning issues covered in Tables 3.1 and 3.2, as well as the questions in Chapter 3 in the section titled Family Culture. An interview can last for various amounts of time, but it will not be less than one hour, and the length will depend largely on the setting. At the end of the interview, be sure to give the family a time for the next meeting.

## *Mapping and Graphic Tools*

The genogram, ecomap, and social network map and grid are valuable mapping and graphic assessment tools. The genogram provides information about the family as a system as well as its internal and external structures. Family of origin, culture, and attachment genograms are commonly used by practitioners (DeMaria, Weeks, & Hof, 1999). The ecomap shows the interactions the family has outside the family environment. Ecomaps reveal the systems in the larger environment by pointing out connections beyond the immediate family. Identifying important relationships—with friends, relatives, church, schools, social groups, organizations, work, and other life settings—gives the practitioner and family a sense of current environmental connections to other systems. The social network map and grid capture the family behavior in the context of its social network and social support—emotional support, concrete support, and informational support. They allow a pictorial assessment of needed resources for the family.

*The Family Genogram* The intergenerational family genogram collects and organizes data along genealogical lines. Information depicting the family along intergenerational and historical lines is drawn using symbols. With these symbols, a practitioner can display various details of a family such as family history; current family membership; events such as births, deaths, miscarriages, adoptions, separations, divorces, education, illnesses; and other relevant information about the family that will be valuable in assessment.

Pictorial representation is used to show practical and comprehensive information in key areas of individual and family functioning, such as the family structures, boundaries, and composition within the context of family generations. Data are then added to help explain the family structure, history, and process, which can reveal key intergenerational themes and patterns, relational patterns, and developmental issues in the family (DeMaria, Weeks, & Hof, 1999).

Genograms can illustrate many different aspects of the family patterns. A family genogram may be drawn to show intergenerational relationships, cultural identity, conflicts and supports, and traditions and rituals; it can highlight issues such as alcoholism, corporal punishment, child abuse, adoptions, and other concerns

**Table 4.1** Questions for the First Family Interview

**WHO**

Who is a member of this family?

Who is experiencing the concerns?

Who is most/least concerned about the problem?

Who is most affected/least affected by the concerns?

Who brought the family here?

**WHAT**

What is the concern that brings you here?

What meaning does the problem have for each of you?

What solutions have you attempted?

What perpetuates the concerns/problems?

What are the family beliefs about what maintains the problem?

What are the problems that perpetuate the beliefs?

What does the family do if there is/is no change?

**WHY**

Why is the family coming for assistance now?

Why is it important that the family change?

**WHERE**

Where did the information about the problem come from?

Where does the family view the problem as originating?

**WHEN**

When did the problem begin?

When does the problem occur? When does the problem not occur?

**HOW**

How might the family look, behave, or feel without the problem/concerns?

How might the family relationships change without the concerns?

How does a change in the individual affect others?

How does the family maintain the concern/problem?

How will the family know when the concern/problem is not present?

How might this practitioner constrain/prevent the family from finding their own solution?

*Source: Adapted from* Nurses and Families: A Guide to Family Assessment and Intervention. *Second Edition, by L. Wright and M. Leahey. Copyright © 1994 F. A. Davis. Adapted by permission.*

about any family through the generations. Genograms provide a snapshot in time, and recreating them as treatment proceeds can be very revealing.

*Constructing the Genogram*    In using genograms, social workers should be aware of several cautions concerning their interpretation. "Some studies suggest that there is actually very limited agreement among clinicians on using genogram symbols, and the symbols used do not describe the diversity of family interaction. The symbols focus primarily on closeness, distance, and conflict patterns in families"

(DeMaria, Weeks, & Hof, 1999, p. 7). There are no standardized symbols for recording child abuse, addiction patterns, or family violence. The practitioner should indicate through the use of a legend on the genogram what each symbol stands for. With a well-explained symbol system, genograms can help organize family information in qualitative and quantitative ways.

The usual practice is to draw three generations of the family showing family composition, structure, relationships, and other information over time. Family members are placed on horizontal rows to signify a generation, such as a marriage or co-habitation. Children are represented by vertical lines and rank-ordered from left to right beginning with the eldest child. Males are denoted by squares and females by circles. See the blank genogram in Figure 4.1 and the common genogram symbols Figure 4.2.

Names and ages, usually birthdates, appear in the square or circle. Just outside the circle or box, important information can be placed, such as an illness, problem, or reason for death. Other noteworthy comments can be used such as mental health diagnosis. An example of the Joe Smith family genogram is shown in Figure 4.3 drawn with the markings and symbols from Figure 4.2.

At the beginning of a family interview, tell the family you will be asking them questions about their background that are important for gaining a picture of the family and their situation. Using a large piece of paper, draw the genogram allowing everyone to see what you are recording, explaining what the symbols mean as you draw. As you continue collecting information you may even ask family members to draw symbols and write comments on the genogram. Start by drawing a square and a circle with the family before you. Let the members know that you are interested in family composition and boundaries. It is often very enlightening to everyone in the group to hear about family members in detail.

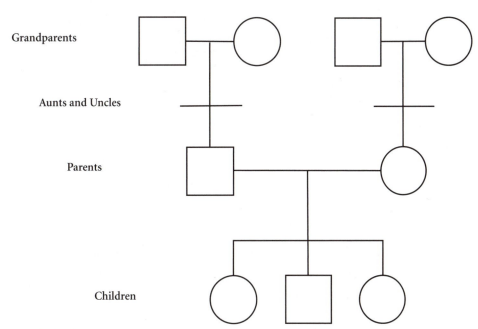

**Figure 4.1** Blank Genogram

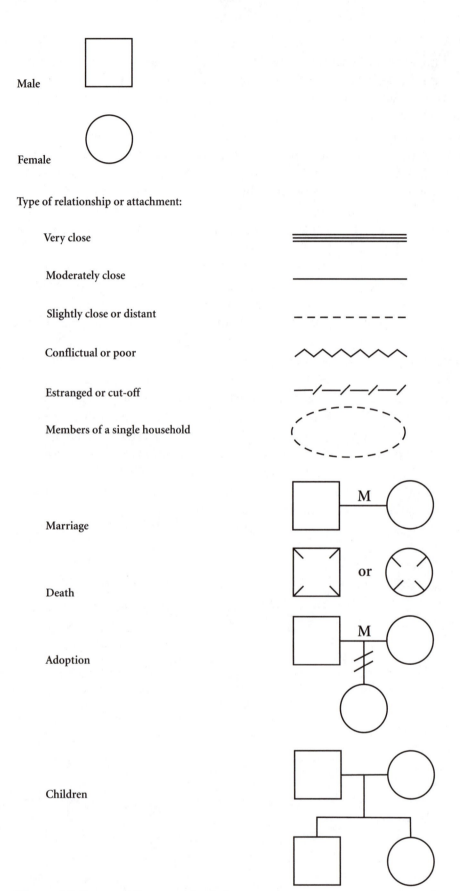

Male

Female

Type of relationship or attachment:

Very close

Moderately close

Slightly close or distant

Conflictual or poor

Estranged or cut-off

Members of a single household

Marriage

Death

Adoption

Children

**Figure 4.2** Common Genogram Symbols

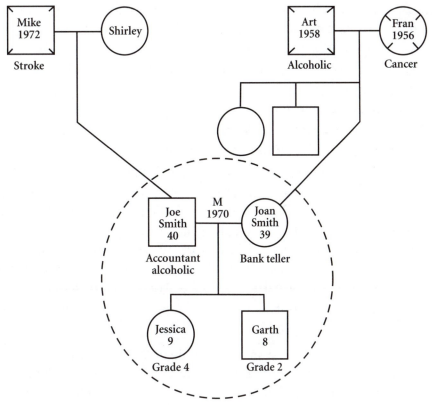

**Figure 4.3** The Joe Smith Family Genogram

To assist the family in feeling comfortable with information collection, you may find the following practice guidelines to be helpful.

1. Collect as much information as possible about the family's membership by drawing three generations.
2. Provide the opportunity for the family to go back at the end of the interview and comment on the genogram or add information that they did not at first include.
3. Remember that the individuals in the family are the experts on their family system.
4. The genogram may be referred to as a family tree.
5. The family provides whatever information they are comfortable with and can decline to answer any question they do not have information about or do not wish to address. You can always return to the genogram and probably should in later sessions. Update the information in later sessions, comparing the new entries to material in the original genogram.
6. Let the family members tell you, or draw for you, members of their family in the order they choose.
7. Colored markers or crayons can be used to enhance the genogram in a way that makes it the family's interpretation.
8. Start with the least threatening questions about family structure, membership, and where family members live before asking about health and mental illnesses, and other matters requiring greater cooperation.

9. If the family is having difficulty remembering dates, help them by asking questions such as, How old might you have been? Were you in high school? What season of the year was it?

10. Ask questions that help the family to think about themselves in relation to their family, such as,

    "Whom are you most like?"

    "Whom are you least like? Why?"

    "Who would you call if you had a problem?"

    "Who would you like to call if you had a problem?"

11. Start with the immediate family members before going into the extended family. The amount of detail gathered about the extended family will depend on the family's difficulties, and this is a clinical judgment. It is usual to alternate between wife and husband when asking about each spouse's family of origin. This allows both to contribute to the session. Avoid getting sidetracked and overwhelmed with information.

12. Draw a circle around the members of the current household to distinguish them.

Most families are interested in viewing their family through the genogram. This will probably be the first time they have ever seen their family information organized in this fashion. Therefore, it may be overwhelming, or it may trigger emotions that they had not expressed, or it may initiate discussions about their own problems and family. Practitioners need to be aware of the range of reactions families can have to their genogram; and they must be prepared to use the genogram for both collecting and organizing data and for helping families make connections to significant events and issues within their family system. It has been suggested that the family genogram provides four times as much social, health, family history, and family structural and relational patterns as interviews (Wright & Leahey, 1994).

*The Ecomap*   Another way to represent the family's interaction with various systems is by drawing an ecomap. Ecomaps depict systems the family interacts with and indicates where changes may be needed with the environmental systems to provide improved interactions and supports for a family. Information about the family's social context is shown using squares or circles to represent social support. In these graphic pictures the practitioner can see where supportive relationships exist and where deficiencies and areas of conflict appear. Are there missing connections or interfaces that need to be changed? Is social isolation a problem? Ecomaps indicate the flow of resources between the family and other significant people, agencies, and organizations that may be supporting or stressing the family environment. Ecomaps help determine the resources and interventions necessary for resolution of many family stressors.

*Constructing the Ecomap*   Start by explaining to the family that you wish to obtain a picture of their current situation. Place the family household in the center of the paper as a circle. Label the family within the circle. Around the family household, draw circles to indicate the family's environment such as work, day care, school, extended family, church, recreation, friends of family, friends of children, drinking buddies, and others as appropriate for the family. The circles can be drawn any size. Lines are drawn to show the quality of the relationships with the connections. Common depictions are (1) straight lines for strong connections—and the wider the line, the stronger the connection; (2) dotted lines for tenuous relationships; (3) slashed lines for stressful relationships; and (4) arrows to indicate the flow of the relationship between the systems. These can be drawn in both directions and one way.

Ecomaps highlight the types of relationships families want inside their family structure and outside the immediate family. Ecomaps should be drawn at various points over time to indicate change. Drawing ecomaps at the beginning of family work and again after intervention provides a picture of the changing relationships in the family's environment. Ecomaps allow families to understand both the process and the patterns that have developed with the family and its environment. Genograms and ecomaps can be used with all families. Three ecomaps are included here: Figure 4.4, which shows a blank ecomap; and Figure 4.5, which shows the Smith family ecomap; and Figure 4.6, which shows a child's ecomap.

*Social Network Map and Grid*   Social networks are patterns depicting the personal relationships that sustain each individual by helping him or her cope with the usual demands of daily living and the impact of serious stressful situations. Connections between people in a social network can be described as a set of relationships—represented as links in a chain—and can become quite complex. Social network maps help us identify the number of people available to support a family.

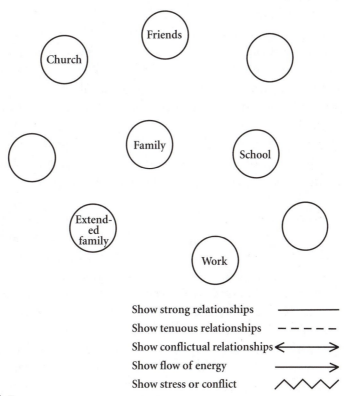

**Figure 4.4** Blank Ecomap

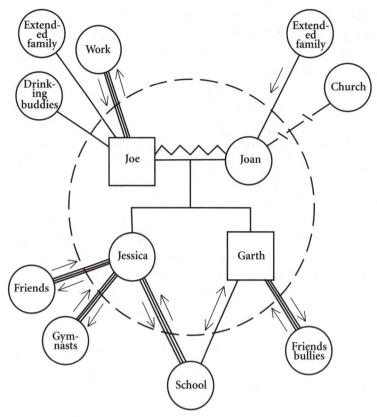

**Figure 4.5** Smith Family Ecomap

A social network grid can document other aspects of a social network, such as the categories of informal social support provided, their frequency, and their reliability.

One way to envision informal supports for families is to imagine a social network as a convoy—a group of people who travel alongside us, protecting and escorting us through life. The size of the convoy, the kinds of people within it, and the degree to which people in it are close and available to help us over the course of our life will vary form person to person. Over a lifetime, members of your convoy change: Some people drop out, some relationships become closer, others grow more distant, and a few remain stable and consistent (Gammonley & Thomlison, 2000).

Families who have few close relationships in earlier years are less likely to have adequate informal supports as they get older. There can be a number of contributing factors: recent immigration to the United States, personal disability for some or all of the adult life, chronic mental illness or substance abuse, or the strains associated with caring for a child while struggling to cope with adult responsibilities. Families with fewer supports also may be less likely to have provided help to others. Whatever the reason, some families, when confronted with challenges and crisis, may have a much smaller and weaker informal social network available to assist them. Families who have adequate support networks are generally better able to get through crises and difficulties than are those who must confront their problems with no external help.

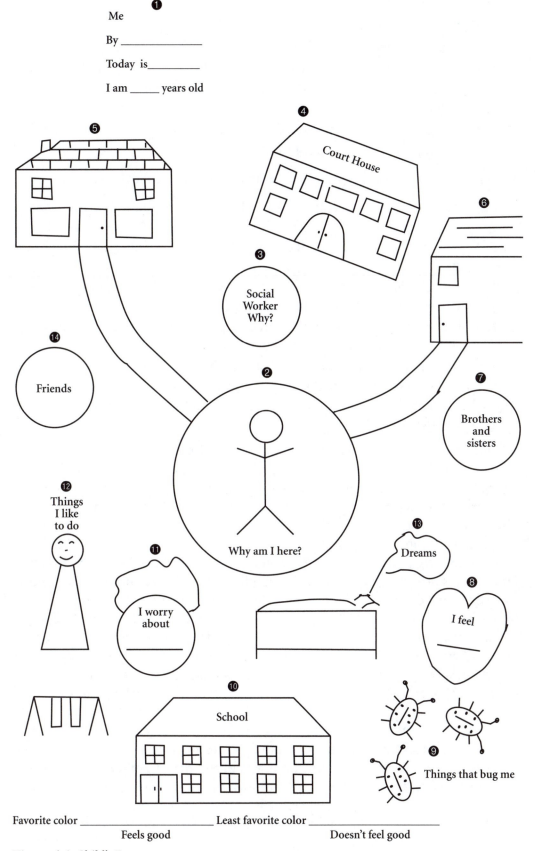

**Figure 4.6** Child's Ecomap

Support helps families in many ways:

- Reducing social isolation
- Increasing knowledge of community resources
- Offering an opportunity to learn and practice problem-solving skills
- Allowing modeling and practice of family communication skills
- Providing companionship
- Providing emotional support during times of crisis
- Enhancing self-esteem and coping

Questions for exploring social support in the family include these:

1. What is the family's history of providing informal social support to other people as well as its own members?
2. What is the family's experience of receiving support from other people and family members?
3. What is the current physical and mental health status of the family members and dependent children?
4. What are the demands of the caregiving role that impact the range and number of persons in the social support network?
5. Is the family receiving "negative" informal social support? "Negative" social support is assistance provided by friends, neighbors, and family members that is not wanted and has been demonstrated to be actually harmful to the well-being of the family.

*Constructing the Social Network Map and Grid*   To construct a social network, draw a circle and divide it into seven sections; label these work/school, organizations/church, friends, neighbors, formal services, household, and other family. To assess the presence of social support for a family, first ask the family members to identify all members of their network. List the names of each individual under one or more of the appropriate sections. Use of the social network grid can help the practitioner assess the quality and amount of support provided by each named individual. For each person listed, the family member describes (1) the kind of support provided, such as emotional, concrete, informational; (2) the degree to which the individual is critical to the family member; (3) the direction of help provided to or by the family member; (4) the degree of closeness perceived by the family member; and (5) the frequency of contact and the length of the relationship. Use the results to evaluate intervention and resource needs. See Figure 4.7 for an example of the Social Network Map and Figure 4.8 for the Social Network Grid.

## Self-Report Tools

Incorporating standardized measures into the assessment and intervention process requires deciding what will be measured, when, and how. Chapter 6 discusses this matter in greater detail. Deciding what to measure is primarily grounded in what the family considers important. Essentially you are trying to measure an issue or problem and whether it changes over time. Standardized tools measure these types of change:

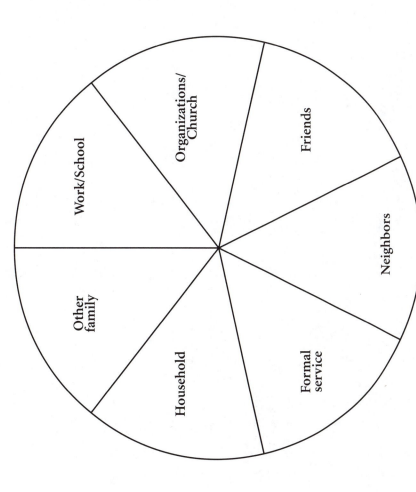

**Instructions:**

This version of the Social Network map is used to assess the presence of social support for the family.

**Step 1:**

Sit with the family while completing this form. Ask the family members to name all individuals in their social network.

**Step 2:**

List the names of each individual under the appropriate section.

**Step 3:**

Use the Social Network Grid to assess the quality and amount of support provided by each named individual.

**Figure 4.7** Social Network Map (*Source: From "The Social Network Map: Assessing Social Support in Clinical Practice," by E. M. Tracy and J. K. Whittaker, 1990, Families in Society, pp. 463, 466. Copyright © 1990 Family Service America. Reprinted by permission.*)

**Instructions:** Use the first column of the grid to record the name of each person listed on the Social Network Map. For each person listed, ask the family member to describe the kind of support provided (concrete, emotional, information/advice), the degree to which an individual is critical of the family member, the direction of help provided to and/or provided by the family member, the degree of closeness perceived by the family member, and the frequency of contact and length of the relationship.

| Name | Areas of Life | Concrete Support | Emotional Support | Information/ Advice | Critical of your activities? | Direction of help provided? | Closeness | How often do you see them? | How long have you known them? |
|---|---|---|---|---|---|---|---|---|---|
| | 1. Household<br>2. Other family<br>3. Work/school<br>4. Organizations<br>5. Other friends<br>6. Neighbors<br>7. Professionals<br>8. Other | 1. Hardly ever<br>2. Sometimes<br>3. Almost always | 1. Hardly ever<br>2. Sometimes<br>3. Almost always | 1. Hardly ever<br>2. Sometimes<br>3. Almost always | 1. Hardly ever<br>2. Sometimes<br>3. Almost always | 1. Goes both ways.<br>2. You to them.<br>3. They to you. | 1. Not very close.<br>2. Sort of close.<br>3. Very close. | 0. Does not see.<br>1. Few times per year<br>2. Monthly<br>3. Weekly<br>4. Daily | 1. Less than than 1 year.<br>2. 1–5 years<br>3. > 5 years |

**Figure 4.8** Social Network Grid (*Source: From "The Social Network Map: Assessing Social Support in Clinical Practice," by E. M. Tracy and J. K. Whittaker, 1990, Families in Society, pp. 463. Copyright © 1990 Family Service America. Reprinted by permission.*)

- Change in *circumstances,* such as decreased conflict
- Change in *attitude,* such as increased self-respect and family identity
- Change in *skills,* such as increased parenting skills
- Change in *behavior,* such as increased contact with a parent or increased sibling contact of a positive nature

Two general methods or approaches to self-report measures are identified in the literature: (1) the use of standardized tools and (2) the use of pragmatic indicators. Standardized self-report tools include tests, questionnaires, rating scales, checklists, inventories, or any instrument that is systematically used between the family and practitioner. These measures will have uniform administration and scoring procedures resulting in increased assurance that you are measuring what you think you are measuring.

Pragmatic self-report indicators rely largely on family self-statements. These tools, such as journals, logs, and self-anchored scales, are considered less efficient and more prone to bias than standardized instruments, but they can elicit important qualitative information about family functioning. Family members record their thoughts, feelings, and behaviors with these tools. For example, you may ask a wife to record the number of times she has thought about having sexual relations with her husband, or wanting to leave the marriage. These statements can create a baseline for how frequently a problem occurs by measuring the thoughts, feelings, or behaviors of family members. This is done by collecting information from them through the use of a chart, journal, or log recording technique. Self-recording has both practical and clinical relevance in family work and is compatible with interviewing, mapping and other graphic depictions, and standardized forms of measurement.

*Self-Anchored Rating Scales*   To measure a problem using a self-anchored or rating scale, the family and practitioner construct a scale that is specific to the family situation. Descriptors are developed to measure or rate the problem or concern. For example, a scale may be constructed to measure the family's morning communication skills and is completed by each family member (see Figure 4.9).

The numbers represent measures of improvement and are used to monitor progress and change. Families are fond of these measures because they are simple to understand and use, and the family members can participate in the development of the anchors.

Rating lists can be constructed for specific problems such as communication skills: talking for self, listening to others, asking questions, asking questions without interrupting, summarizing messages. Scales can be developed to rate each skill from 1 (very clear) to 5 (not very clear at all). Self-anchored and rating scales provide ways to quantify problems that are meaningful to the family situation. These are not rigorous measures because they have not been scientifically developed. They are meaningful, however, to both the practitioner and the family; sometimes they are the best available tool for a particular problem situation.

## Teaching and Role-Play Tools

Observing behavior is one of the most common ways of collecting information on individual and family behaviors. It is time-consuming and often not practical, but behavior occurring in the meeting can certainly be observed, as can behavior in

**Instructions:** Circle the number that best describes your morning behavior on a scale of 1 to 5, with 1 showing unacceptable or uncooperative behavior at home in the morning and 5 showing excellent or cooperative behavior in getting ready in the morning. Where are you on the scale?

| | **Unacceptable** | | | **Excellent** | |
| | Slow to get up; refuses to dress; does not eat with others | | | Pleasant; rises quickly; dresses; eats with others | |
|---|---|---|---|---|---|
| Monday | 1 | 2 | 3 | 4 | 5 |
| Tuesday | 1 | 2 | 3 | 4 | 5 |
| Wednesday | 1 | 2 | 3 | 4 | 5 |
| Thursday | 1 | 2 | 3 | 4 | 5 |
| Friday | 1 | 2 | 3 | 4 | 5 |
| Saturday | 1 | 2 | 3 | 4 | 5 |
| Sunday | 1 | 2 | 3 | 4 | 5 |

**Figure 4.9** Family Morning Cooperation Skills

the family home environment when the practitioner meets the family there. These times provide opportunities for change in the "moment" as the practitioner teaches or shows the family how to behave differently through coaching, role play, and feedback about the behavior. This typically involves asking the family to perform a task or procedure while a person external to the family evaluates the interaction. Tasks and procedures can be rated systematically or by informal observation means. Behavior is rated by its frequency and duration or both—for example, the number of times you observe that father does not answer mother's questions and tends to turn his head away. The practitioner or family member can record the frequency of a behavior, or time its duration.

Role plays assist family members to practice and experience behaviors and feelings in nonthreatening situations. Essentially the persons have an opportunity to rehearse behaviors and responses. Repeated practice opportunities with feedback from family members and the practitioner can often result in the newly learned responses being integrated into daily functioning behaviors and patterns. Practicing communication skills, job-interviewing skills, parent-child requests, and other behaviors over a period of time can help family members improve those skills. Improvements can be documented through self-monitoring methods, such as logs and journals, or through videotape. Learning occurs with repetition, and the role play can be used for both assessment and measures of change in behavior.

## *Issues of Concern*

The main issue in collecting data and assessing the family system is to gain an accurate picture of family strengths and problems in order to create appropriate matches between needs of the family and services offered to them. Moreover, because of the demands for service, it is important to attend to those families with the most immediate need, and with an acceptable level of service intensity. Families with lower levels of need can receive less intensive, less restrictive service, and less intrusive levels of service delivery. Finally, structured family assessment instruments can assist with practitioner consistency. As practitioners are faced with more and more complex social, clinical, and administrative conditions, the application of a multidimensional family assessment measure can promote consistency in interpretation of problems and decision making in similar types of cases.

## Culturally Sensitive Assessment

American families are culturally and racially diverse. The richness of family culture will be evident only by exploring such factors as varying expectations and attitudes resulting from ethnic, religious, cultural, racial, and gender differences. These factors may shape your ability to form a trusting relationship with families. You will want to be aware of your own expectations, communication patterns, and responses to power and authority. Failure to address your sense of being different may cause unwillingness among the family members to be open with you and thus interfere with the establishment of a helping relationship. Such factors will differ in families depending on culture and your ease in exploring these through your relationship, but in some families there may be subjects that are controversial, taboo, or simply provocative.

Many families will view you, the helper, with caution, particularly if you are from the dominant culture. In many situations it is best to match worker and family culturally. If you are a member of a minority group working with families from your own culture, you may be the best person to understand their difficulties from a culturally competent perspective.

The complexity of these differences creates challenges. The challenge for the practitioner is to discern, validate, and simplify the complexity. For practitioners to work successfully with culturally diverse families, McGill (1992, p. 339) believes that they

1. Need to have knowledge of the particular content of many different cultures;
2. Need to be able to make the presence of differences with the family, between the family and the therapist, and between the family and the larger societal system an opportunity rather than a problem; and
3. Need to hear the complexity of the family's story within the context of society's stories in a way that simplifies the story for ordinary daily family life.

## Selecting Dimensions for Assessment

As a fact-finding method that gathers pertinent information about a family system, assessment should include a quantitative measure as part of the process. The purpose of measuring family problems and resources are the following:

1. *Quantifying family problems.* Practitioners can focus on the most critical areas of child, family, and environmental functioning. When the severity of problems or factors facing family members is determined, interventions can

be allocated so that more time and resources are being spent on those family concerns, that are most problematic.

2. *Supporting and improving clinical judgment.* Measuring family behavior guides practitioners in developing case plans that specifically address the most pressing concerns. Measurement adds to the quality of information on which practitioners base their clinical decisions.

3. *Providing a common and consistent perspective to problems.* Through documentation of information provided by a qualitative measure of assessment, family problems can be reassessed over the course of service. All measures should be given at the beginning (pretest) and at the end of the intervention (posttest). Follow-up is also desirable. In this way, monitoring and evaluation of change and family functioning is determined. Reassessing the same factors makes it possible to determine the progress a family has made in reducing problems. From these data, relevant and timely plans for a family can be made.

4. *Determining the appropriate level of service.* Using a quantitative measure with clinical interviewing, practitioners can identify the key factors that must be addressed through intervention. By developing baseline indicators of family functioning, practitioners can base decisions on objective criteria and recognize family strengths in culturally appropriate ways.

The use of family measures can be adversely affected by the following five issues: (1) practitioner or system misuse of instruments; (2) inadequate practitioner knowledge and skill; (3) poor reliability and validity of the instrument; (4) use of an inappropriate instrument; and (5) use of an instrument in an inappropriate context, in that not all cases will be amenable to quantification.

A combination of tools for collecting information and evaluating family change is desirable. In determining which tools to use, consider the following:

- Start with this question: What information is needed?
- Choose a measure that is simple, practical, and meaningful to the family.
- Measure one or two things well.
- Involve the family in defining the outcomes to measure.
- Review the measure with the family who will be using it.
- Build on what the family is prepared to document. Do not overwhelm the family.
- Collect multiple and repeated measures.

Remember that using family measures is not an end in itself but an important way in which you and the family can gain clarity about the focus of change, and a way for both of you to know when change has occurred. The success or failure of measurement depends on how you present the measurement task to the family.

Fischer and Corcoran (1994) have compiled a list of measures for adults, children, and couples related to a number of psychological, behavioral, and interpersonal difficulties. The measures have been reproduced in their book, and you can examine them to find one suitable for the family's concerns.

# Summary of Key Practice Principles

Key practice principles in the use of measurement tools for family assessment include the following (Thomlison & Bradshaw, 1999, p. 174):

1. Be familiar with how the measurement works. Try the task yourself first and practice on friends or colleagues. Know how it works and how long it will take to complete.

2. Assure the family of the importance, purpose, and use of the information obtained from the measure. One of the most important messages that a practitioner can convey to the family is that you have confidence in the value or importance of obtaining the family's responses.

3. Reassure the family that there are no right or wrong answers. Always stress accuracy and honesty.

4. Review the entire measurement task with the family before they need to complete it on their own. Be sensitive to the educational, social, and cultural background of the family, such as reading and language difficulties. Remember that the objective of measurement is to obtain information that will assist you and your family to evaluate progress towards goal achievement.

5. Review the results with the family. Explain the significance of and/or how you will use the results. This shows respect for the family and decreases the "expert mystique" of the practitioner.

6. Use the individual items or details provided by the measurement task to discuss strengths as well as areas for further development. Do not just use the total score or gross outcome. Remember, all measurement needs to be simple, practical, unobtrusive, culturally appropriate, and of importance to family and practitioner.

# Learning Activities

## Activity 4.1: Role Play — The First Interview

The goal of the first interview is to build an alliance with the family and to develop a hypothesis about what is happening in the family. Divide the class into two or three groups, and have some students role-play a family visiting a practitioner for the first interview. Students role-playing the family should use one of the cases in the book to develop the problem and issues. One student assumes the role of the practitioner and the others will observe and provide feedback on the role-play objectives. The task is to introduce yourself, meet family members, and orient the family to the room and to the session—for example, explain who you are, what will happen, how long will you need, what paperwork is involved, how confidentiality will be handled, and what the purpose of the family meeting is. Collect information from each member of the family on what brought the group to counseling. Use the questions from Table 4.1 to guide the role play.

Be sure to learn from the family their experience on what other challenges they have faced and how they resolved these issues. If you don't find a balance between difficulties and strengths, the problems may feel overwhelming to the family. It is useful to ask what strategies have been attempted to solve the problem in the past. Often the problem is being maintained by efforts to resolve it. Frequently stragtegies have been tried but were not pursued long enough to have an effect. Use 30 minutes for the activity and after you finish the session, the student practitioner will identify the hypothesis, the strengths, and the issues in the family. With classmates and role players, discuss the hypothesis and how well you conducted the first interview. Is the assessment accurate? What other suggestions for questions or techniques may have generated more family information?

## Activity 4.2: Genogram—Assessing the Impact of Culture

Assess your family system and family culture. To understand and assess the role of uniqueness and culture in your family system, draw a three-generation family cultural genogram. Use any of the symbols suggested in the chapter or devise your own to illustrate cultural aspects of your family system. Use colors, pictures, stickers, or any other symbols to designate unique aspects of your family system culture. Bring the genogram to class and discuss how these influences are part of you today or have impacted you. In what ways do you think your cultural influences may affect your work with families? List the ways your culture may be a barrier or strength in working with a family.

## Activity 4.3: Case Study—Sources of Support

Select one of the cases in the book and examine the sources of social support for that family using the social network map and grid. Based on one area of support— for example, concrete, emotional, or informational support—what thoughts or conclusions can you draw from using this assessment tool? Use the information in this chapter to guide your assessment. Now, what three things would you do (intervention) to assist this family based on the social support information?

▼▼▼

# CHAPTER FIVE

# *Family Interventions*

An intervention is a specific set of activities and accompanying skills developed to prevent a problem or to promote, improve, or sustain functioning and the factors that contribute to it (Corcoran, 1992). Effective family interventions are often empirically based strategies shown to be helpful for the type of difficulty occurring in the presenting family. Matching the interventions to the family's issues and concerns is very important. In general, data suggest that family-centered strategies are effective in modifying family and child relational functioning. Addressing risk factors and providing protection from them can have powerful change effects.

Think about what goes on during daily family life within the presenting problem framework; you will see that problems can generally be addressed through strategies of parenting (caregiving), teaching, supporting, providing, and relating. Your next task is to combine these observations with data from the assessment and plan the most appropriate intervention.

## *Planning for an Intervention*

The family system should be organized for stability; when its structure is threatened, the family's sense of stability is threatened. Any change from outside or inside the family system has the potential to disrupt it. Change, as was noted, is both positive and negative, and families learn to cope with the stress of change by minimizing disruption and adapting. Problem-solving patterns emerge, and families find solutions to their stressors, for the most part. Thus, habitual patterns arise through which issues and problems can be addressed as a matter of fact.

Sometimes families adhere to their patterns too rigidly, and lack the flexibility to adapt when new problems arise. When families are "stuck" in these patterns, seeking help is a solution to their dilemma. Both the practitioner and the family need to understand the nature of this change process and what prevents the system from making adaptations to stressors.

Families are constantly confronted with the stability-change dilemma. Family practitioners differ in their opinions of how change occurs, but they know that change is ongoing in all families. Change does not always come from internal family sources; interactions with various systems outside the family can be change factors. As someone external to the family, the practitioner can also serve as a catalyst for change.

Change can occur within individuals in the family, and within the family structure itself. Change in family members is often called "first-order" change. First-order change is quantitative, gradual, and continuous and does not exceed the rules of the family. These changes are temporary and superficial in the family system because they leave the basic family structure and functioning unaltered (Nichols & Schwartz, 1995). Second-order change is more substantial; often abrupt, it involves discontinuity and family structure change. Second-order changes are longer lasting (Nichols & Schwartz, 1995).

As a beginning practitioner, you should probably work on first-order changes, developing family members' inner strengths and beliefs that they can improve their situations—even if the change is modest at first. Small changes can positively affect future family functioning that will extend beyond the direct support of the practitioner and other social systems. It will move you toward the ultimate family goal: greater self-sufficiency and fewer total treatment needs (Thornton, Craft, Dahlberg, Lynch, & Baer, 2000).

All family interventions will fall into one of three areas: cognitive, affective, or behavioral (Thornton, Craft, Dahlberg, Lynch, & Baer, 2000). Interventions can be targeted at any one or all three domains. Many theorists (Alexander & Parsons, 1982; Franklin & Jordan, 1999; Henggeler et al., 1998; Rothery & Enns, 2001; Thyer, 1989; Whittaker, Schinke, & Gilchrist, 1986) agree that the most profound and sustained change will occur through changes in the family's belief system (cognitions). How a family thinks will determine how it functions or behaves. In turn, these changes can affect the way family members relate to and feel about one another.

## Selecting Realistic Goals

One of the most common errors of practitioners is to establish unrealistic goals in an unrealistic time frame for families. Too often they set too many goals and families find it is impossible to reach any of them. Realistic expectations of what can be achieved need to be agreed to early in the relationship and spelled out in a contract with the family. Contracts can be written or verbal, but the goals must be stated explicitly in them and never left only in the "mind" of the practitioner. Vague goals are unachievable goals. Together with the family, establish the goals for treatment based on the problems the families is most concerned with, the resources of the family, and the changes they would like to see.

The contact should describe both the practitioner's role and the family's role in the intervention. Expected gains, benefits, and other outcomes should also be clearly explained, along with costs and time involved.

## Searching for Solutions

When practitioners focus on trying to understand *why* the family system is the way it is, little change will occur. Instead, they should look at the here-and-now. Considering questions as a type of intervention, they should ask *what* is maintaining the problem, *what* is needed to make a change, and most important, *what* can be done to effect a change. These types of questions initiate change in the family system by placing emphasis on family strengths, and they avoid blaming someone or some event for the troubles. Searching for solutions rather than causes is ultimately more useful. Change is initiated when you ask questions that highlight *difference* in the family situation between the way it is now and the way it can be. The family seeks solutions, and self-direction is an important attribute of change. For example, what would be different if Carlos were not asthmatic? What would be different if mom did not work? What would you do differently if dad were to attend your soccer games? Benefits of these questions include the shift in the family's cognitive, affective, and behavioral functioning as they look different, think differently, and begin to feel different about the family and their circumstances.

## Building on Family Strengths

Families have assets, strengths, energy sources and other resources that can help resolve their problems. Helping the family evaluate their strengths permits them to review their resources for solving their own dilemmas. Twelve family strengths are listed here, and this checklist can help practitioners build interventions for family change (Wright & Leahey, 1994, p. 193).

1. Ability to address the physical, emotional, and spiritual needs of family members.
2. Ability to be sensitive to family members.
3. Ability to communicate through thoughts and feelings.
4. Ability to provide security, support, and encouragement.
5. Ability to initiate and maintain growth-producing relationships and experiences within and without the family.
6. Capacity to maintain and create constructive and responsible community relationships.
7. Ability to perform family roles flexibly.
8. Ability for self-help and to accept help when appropriate.

9. Capacity for mutual respect for the individuality of family members.
10. Ability to use a crisis experience as a means of growth—a challenge.
11. Concern for family unity, loyalty, and interfamily cooperation.
12. Ability to grow with and through children.

## Changing Cognitive Thinking

Good intervention questions generate new ideas, opinions, or information about problem solving or behavior change. They focus on the connections between the ways families think, feel, and act solving problems. The intent is to change a family's perceptions and beliefs about a problem or behavior. You can help families change the way they process information by changing the kinds of questions you ask. This can guide them toward thinking about their circumstances and solutions in a new light. Productive intervention questions may include these (Wright & Leahy, 1994, p. 105):

1. *Survival* questions—How have you managed to survive?
2. *Support* questions—What people have given you special understanding? How did you find them?
3. *Exception* questions—When things were going well in life, what was different?
4. *Possibility* questions—What are your hopes, visions, and aspirations?
5. *Esteem* questions—What are people likely to say about your good qualities? What about your life gives you real pride? How will you know when things are going well in your life?

When families stop and think about your questions, they can see that they have attained accomplishments, and their past coping is a form of strength, giving them relevant competencies to build on. As they change their view of themselves, they are frequently able to see solutions to their difficulties. Two techniques that can help with this are reframing and teaching.

*Reframing* Turning problems into strengths requires practitioners to reframe family problems into abilities, a technique frequently used in family practice. This is accomplished by keeping the focus on individual and family strengths rather than on problems and pathology. Reframing an issue or problem by relabeling a family's description of a behavior shifts the conceptual or informational view of the situation and changes the meaning and thinking associated with a situation or behavior. The new meaning is a more acceptable one: for example, describing a mother as loving rather than nosey; describing an adolescent as depressed rather than lazy; describing a young child as energetic and motivated rather than bad.

*Teaching* Very often, both children and adults in families can benefit from education or information about a problem or way of handling a problem. Families develop myths about an illness or behavior, and parent skills, child development information, or health education can teach families how new information and information processing affects their behavior. Changing behavior changes beliefs. Families learn strategies for recognizing and regulating feelings, and through modeling and coaching practice, they learn to apply new skills. Many times, education and information are not sufficient, and in these situations coaching, mentoring, and parent-child management in the form of parent training are necessary. These interventions are effective if applied in the early stages of most child problems and when parents are engaged in parent-training activities for a prolonged period of time. Parents in the most need and with the most difficult child, such as one showing early signs of aggression, are also the parents who are most difficult to retain in these approaches (Corcoran, 2000; Mulvey, Arthur, & Reppucci, 2000). To effect change with these families, practitioners must be persistent and patient.

## Changing Affective Factors

The emotional state of families influences their abilities to deal with problems. While many factors contribute to the way family members feel and the affect they display in certain situations, their reactions are often related to their lives—and they frequently reflect the stress and disorder of poverty, past experiences of trauma, or other contextual factors that are discouraging and overwhelming. There may be specific psychological diagnoses among one or more family members—diagnoses such as anxiety disorders or depression. Some family members may have deeply ingrained but unproductive ways of responding to conflict, such as being quick to withdraw, or quick to become angry and leave the room. Emotional states play an important role in how people process information, and this affects their problem solving. Families need to recognize that what they feel, what they say and do or don't do, affects others. Help individuals shift their focus through role playing with family members with whom they have emotional or interpersonal difficulties, this can help them see the issue from the other person's perspective.

Practitioners can help families see the connections between feelings and behaviors. A wife may feel isolated because her husband does not involve her in family decision making. Her sense that she is undervalued may express itself as anger toward her husband on many levels. The practitioner can help her identify her feelings when she is left out of family decisions and clarify what is needed to effect a change. The practitioner must also help the husband realize that listening to others' concerns and feelings develops support and competencies throughout the family unit. Developing support in families is important to changing emotional and affectional states and building positive relations.

## Changing Behaviorial Factors

Most problems in families concern behaviors. Behavior is regulated through both the cognitive and behavioral processes. This is important information for practitioners because it has direct implications for practice. Behavior and affect problems in families are the result of faulty or distorted thinking or belief systems, which contribute to inappropriate behaviors. That is, family problems are translated into behaviors. Behaviors are observable, measurable, and changeable. Change is accomplished through altering what happens before and after the specified behavior occurs. There is a large number of reinforcing and aversive events in any family situation, and identifying current and alternative triggers for the target behavior is the first step in changing it.

Initially, you must determine who has the problem (for example, father and son), what the difficulty is or what needs to be changed (father never spends time with son), and when the problem occurs (after dinner). The family system involved in the interaction must acknowledge the difficulty, confirm the context in which it occurs, and then agree on aspects of the relationship that need change. Information or cues from the father to the son may be misinterpreted as "I don't want to spend time with you." This is in part based on their prior experiences and characteristics. If the father has a history of always going to sleep on the couch after dinner and becoming angry if someone wakes him, then the son is likely to avoid his father, act rejected and angry, and interpret his father's behavior as negative toward him. You will need to help the family imagine a number of possible solutions or behavioral responses to the presenting interaction, a process called generating alternatives. From these, father and son will choose a solution or alternative to the situation. Then the parent and son will need to practice or rehearse the interaction to learn how to modify their existing behavior. Both may need assistance in expressing appropriate and effective responses. After the role-play interaction, the father and son should analyze their behavior and reformulate other responses, if necessary. Role play, rehearsal, and coaching are techniques to address behavior change. Be sure to critique both the content of what is said or performed and the way it is presented (actions).

Devising rituals can assist families in developing new behaviors. Daily rituals, such as bedtime reading with father; yearly rituals, such as celebrating each family member's successes; and cultural rituals, such as eating an ethnic meal dressed in traditional clothes can all improve the family environment. Rituals do not always need to have a celebratory purpose; sometimes they can be created to provide clarity in a family system (DeMaria, Weeks, & Hof, 1999). Suppose parents cannot agree on parenting practices and often give conflicting messages to their children. Confusion is the message received by the children, and this may exacerbate any problem behaviors they are exhibiting. Introducing a ritual of odd-day and even-day parenting may reduce the chaos. Mother may assume care of the children on odd days with father taking care of them on even-numbered days. On Sundays, both parents could share the responsibility and not comment on the other's parenting. This ritual can help the family to develop a routine and understand the impact of their behavior (Wright & Leahey, 1994).

## Creating Opportunities

Regardless of how family problems manifest themselves, complex problems are embedded in psychosocial systems—primarily the family and community. These multisystemic influences shape the family, and change efforts will be affected by these interactions. Be aware of systems in the community such as schools, hospitals, and other agencies with which the family is involved. Each of these systems operates within a practice and policy context, and their larger context can produce information that may be conflicting and confusing to the family; their services may replace the family's own resources (Henggeler et al., 1998; Imber Coppersmith, 1983; Rothery & Enns, 2001), leaving the family feeling inadequate. Practitioners should also examine carefully the environment of the family—its cultural milieu, biculturalism, ethnic status, language, social class, customs, history, and sexual orientation. Creating opportunities for supporting the family in these social systems can help return resources and control to the family system.

Practitioners must understand that both positive and negative family behaviors influence and are influenced by multiple systems internally and externally. Understanding and comparing the values and attitudes of the multisystems interacting with the family system are critical and necessary practitioner tasks. In order to serve families, the practitioner and the systems interacting with families must be free of personal, policy, and practice biases that have a tendency to force families into unproductive patterns (Henggeler et al., 1998). These multiple systems can undermine, thwart, or even inhibit change within a family if they are not working together. The creative use of the family's own resources cannot emerge if barriers impede the family members' opportunities for growth and change.

Choosing interventions in multisystems requires consideration of the following information:

1. What are the systems the family is involved with?
2. What is the relationship between the family and the systems?
3. Is the family blamed for their problems by any of the systems they are involved with?
4. What is the perception of the problem from each system's view?
5. How do the family and the systems define the problems? (Imber Coppersmith, 1983).

When the nature of the family's relationships with other systems has been determined, then interventions can be directed at the appropriate systems to address the external elements that must be involved in family change. Within the system relationship, the interventions are based on having the family take responsibility for viewing their resources as an asset and the community services as a support. The family and its members begin to build skills and knowledge that will help them to be self-sufficient and independent of the practitioner.

## Selecting an Intervention

Interventions do not start some time after the relationship is underway; they begin with the first contact the family has with you, continuing through interviewing and on to termination. With so many types of interventions available, how do you choose? Start by reviewing the characteristics of the family and their referred concerns and issues. Also, consider the most appropriate settings for your intervention, based on research about the identified problems of the family. Then review the family goals and objectives. The intervention you choose should satisfy all the requirements you have idnetified. It should also be culturally appropriate. The family must participate in the choice of intervention.

The intent of an intervention is to ensure that the most effective services available are provided to families. But what does this mean, exactly, for the practitioner and family? Corcoran and Videka-Sherman (1992, p. 25) offer this: "You need to fit your practice to the client problem, . . . the client must be prepared for the intervention, and . . . you must specify the purpose of the intervention and provide as much prescriptive, time-limited structure as possible . . . defining [everything] as clearly and concisely as possible in order to replicate the components that facilitate client change." Clearly, families should have the intervention that has been shown to be the most effective in solving their type of difficulty.

There is usually no single intervention that can address all issues in a family because problem behaviors are maintained by multiple factors. Therefore, it is best to consider several interventions or strategies that are coordinated and will complement one another. For example, social skills training for aggressive young children to develop competence in peer play may be complemented with a home visit strategy focused on parent training. These are both evidence-supported interventions to improve social and emotional competence and skills in young children and their families (Thornton et al., 2000). Families have a right to receive the intervention strategy that is noted to be effective, even with the caveat that not all clients are "guaranteed to benefit from" the intervention (Thyer & Wodarski, 1998, p. 13). Carefully consider the interventions based on resources, level of acceptance by the family, and your experience.

Ideally, best practices are based on rigorous evaluations of interventions reported in peer-reviewed literature. However, a number of factors complicate this. First, research in some areas is not well developed and contains few longitudinal and randomized-control studies. Second, while studies have evaluated the outcome of interventions, the effectiveness for various populations requires more research and support. Finally, it is not the intention of this book to discuss interventions, but to suggest strategies based on the empirically tested principles and experience of the application of multisystemic family work for certain common family problems, particularly for settings where time-limited constraints exist. Practitioners have a responsibility to keep abreast of the literature so they will be aware of the most current and effective treatments for various problems and populations. Those who systematically plan and evaluate their own work will greatly improve the accuracy of their clinical judgement in assessment and in monitoring change during the course of intervention (Thyer, 1994; Thomlison, 1984; Tutty, 1990; Corcoran, 1992). The following practice guidelines have evolved from research on intervention outcomes:

- *Planned* systematic efforts at facilitating change lead to more effective outcomes than *unplanned,* informal help for families.
- Intervention of a structured, directed, and time-limited nature is effective.
- Some interventions are better than no interventions.

## *Parent and Family-Based Strategies*

Parent and family-based interventions are strategies that combine parenting skills, education about child development, and skills for improving communication and reducing conflict. Interventions that start early and address the factors in families that could lead to problem behaviors in children can have substantial effect in reducing child problems. This is the type of improved family relations that parent and family-based interventions are designed to accomplish.

Using parent training or parent education strategies with a behavioral focus, for families of children with conduct problems, has substantial empirical support (Corcoran, 2000). Home-based family strategies are highly recommended as the treatment of choice because they allow practitioners to observe and address parenting practices that need modification in the actual setting and time that they occur. Parenting practices and family environment play an important role in the development of conduct difficulties among preschool children. Coercive parenting practices and poor supervision account for about 50% of the conduct problems displayed in fifth-grade children from all reports.

Parent education rests on the following assumptions:

- Conduct problems in young children are formed and maintained by the family environment.
- Parents unknowingly reinforce noncompliant child behaviors or fail to reinforce the behaviors they wish to see more often in the child.
- Coercive parent-child cycles develop when parents use harsh parenting practices (such as corporal punishment) to deal with disruptive or noncompliant behavior in their children.
- Parents can be taught to have greater positive influence on their children's behaviors.
- Parents can be taught to implement and reinforce prosocial conduct in their children.
- Positive parent-child interaction is critical for attachment between parent and child to develop. (Corcoran, 2000)

## Changing Boundaries

Many child-parent subsystem problems involve family system boundaries—that is, the limits between subsystems. The invisible boundaries of family systems can be thought of as barriers holding outsiders out and holding insiders in and setting limits on the kinds of communications that will occur between the subsystems. In an effort to remain stable and respond to various stressors, families can make their boundaries too rigid and unyielding, or they can develop boundaries that are so permeable they fail to define the subsystem sufficiently. Either too rigid or overly flexible boundaries can be maladaptive. For example, the boundaries between parents and children should allow for parental direction and control and no confusion. When the boundaries are too permeable, then children are in control, and the authority is removed from the parent role. To change the boundary separating parent and child, consider the following:

1. What needs to be strengthened? This may mean reinforcing ideas about parenting, providing information and education, and supporting strategies for renegotiating new boundaries.

2. Who must I support to promote the change? A parent who fears loss of power, and a parent who fears losing what little control he or she has, need support. Adding a boundary is necessary when the parent treats all children the same, failing to recognize that they are in different developmental stages. Recognizing that a difference exists between the children, the parents must define a boundary—by implementing a new practice in the family, such as different bedtimes, more responsibility for the older child, or some other way of acknowledging the oldest child. Removing a boundary may also be necessary. An example might be an excessively rigid boundary in the parent subsystem. Marital difficulties may emerge, spilling into the parent-child subsystem. Breaking triangles and forming or rearranging alliances will be necessary.

3. What change is necessary? When changing boundaries, one can make them more rigid or loose, add them, or remove them. This is done by methods called joining with the family (accepting or accommodating to families in order to win their confidence and circumvent resistance), suggesting change, and coaching parents through the process. No matter what you do regarding boundaries, you will be ineffective unless you have joined appropriately with all those who will be influenced by the changes you initiate.

Changing the emotional climate is necessary. The mood of the family will vary from anger to depression to frustration to discouragement. Your task is to identify the mood by acknowledging each member's right to feel this way under the circumstances and then to lighten the load by providing a clear message of hope that something can be done. Regardless of the severity of the difficulties, family systems and their individual members need opportunities to grow, learn, and develop. Asking the family for an inventory of their preferred solutions, action steps, previous attempts at intervention, and the barriers to success keeps the focus on the family system strengths.

## *The Family Assessment Report*

Practitioners may be asked to write up the information from a family assessment in one of several different ways as each agency and instructor will have a preferred way for recording data gathered from a family. Regardless of the headings used, the information should be organized to indicate system problems and strengths in an integrated fashion. The assessment for each of these areas is summarized and the goal for change is recorded. The intervention plan flows from the data and from what you know about the effectiveness of treatment protocols. When you do not have data, it is also wise to record "practitioner impressions" until such time as more information is available to substantiate or change the impressions. Hypotheses can also be recorded and verified later. The following headings are suggested:

**Family Assessment**

1. Specific problems, issues, and concerns
2. Referred by

*Family Structure and Development*

1. Composition, including members of extended family (genogram data)
2. Descriptive data such as ages, marriages, employment
3. Culture, religion

*Family Functioning (attachment and relational systems of family)*

1. Roles
2. Communication
3. Problem solving
4. Beliefs
5. Alliances/coalitions
6. Concrete supports
7. Emotional supports
8. Instrumental supports

*Family Strengths and Problems (structural, developmental, and functional)*

*Individual Strengths and Problems (physical, psychological, and social)*

Marital subsystem, parent-child subsystem, sibling subsystem, individual subsystem

*Summary/Hypothesis*

*Goals*

*Intervention Plan*

*Date of Assessment and Plan for Update and Review*

Remember that the report is a summary and will not contain all the information gleaned from the family meetings. It represents an integration of theory and practice, and it must be written in a professional manner. Interventions are based on the level of family functioning, the practitioner's expertise, and the context of service. Always keep progress notes and record information about the family as it changes.

# Summary of Practice Principles

1. Intervention planning follows logically from the assessment and must address the problems targeted for change.

2. Assessment is ongoing and multifaceted, with a focus on understanding the ways in which behavioral problems function with family relationship systems. Interventions are also ongoing and multipronged, focusing on change in cognitions, affect, and behavior.

3. Understand that you, the practitioner, are an active part of the family system and the construction of change.

4. What you perceive about a family's situation is obtained by the information you have from the family, your experiences, and the literature.

5. Documenting the assessment information is an essential part of creating the plan of action.

## Learning Activities

### Activity 5.1: Exploring Resources

Write your answers to the following questions, and then discuss your responses with your classmates.

1. How similar/dissimilar are the interventions and resources needed among individuals?

   - In exploring your current situation, what might you do to enhance your situation so that you have sufficient psychological, emotional, physical, spiritual, and social resources to succeed in school?

   - Based on your current level of self-awareness and self-understanding, what one issue would you want to explore with a social worker? What can be done differently to change your problem?

2. After thinking about your response to the above questions, what resources do you think families are most likely to require for success?

3. In what ways might practitioners be helpful to families?

▼▼▼

# CHAPTER SIX

# Measuring and Evaluating Family Change

Tools for collecting and organizing data were discussed in Chapter 4, but along with organizing family data, you will need to monitor and evaluate family progress. You and the family will need to know whether improvement has taken place. Information about change helps the family to maintain or increase their motivation and involvement in the process of change. It helps you understand whether specific intervention strategies need to be maintained, adjusted, or stopped and whether goals have been met. This monitoring allows you to determine the effectiveness of the intervention. There are various ways to measure the changes, and regardless of which ones you use, the important point is for you to assess the family's progress. It is best to obtain information about family functioning by gathering data from several perspectives.

## Selecting Measures to Use

Two primary concerns for evaluation of practice are (1) deciding what measure to use and (2) deciding where and when to obtain the measures. Data from multiple perspectives helps to determine *what* types of information you will need to evaluate progress on. You must still decide *how* you will collect the information in a systematic way. Corcoran and Gingerich (1992) identify two ways to obtain this information: by individualized and by standardized measures of family functioning. They recommend that both be used in practice evaluation.

## Individualized Measures

Individualized measures are designed specifically for the family's unique problem or situation of concern. Individualized measures are "tailored" and developed for the personal concerns of the family. They are usually suitable for obtaining daily feedback on the targeted behavior, which can be stated in behavioral terms for ease of observation (Corcoran & Gingerich, 1992, p. 35). Individualized measures were discussed in Chapter 4 under mapping and the self-report tools. As discussed earlier, these individualized tools are not standardized measures, but they do show change, are meaningful to the family and practitioner, and are very easy to use because family members were involved in their development.

## Standardized Measures

Standardized self-report measures or questionnaires provide information based on constructs from various theoretical models of family functioning. These measures provide information about family functioning in comparison to other families on specific areas or problems. Standardized measures help us verify the findings obtained from the individualized measures. These measures are scales and questionnaires that have known reliability and validity and often have been developed or normed for specific populations with clinical problems. It is usual to administer such measures only a few times during treatment, such as before and after the intervention and at some follow-up period. You need to be sure that the administration of the measure is done in a standardized way so you can be certain that you are measuring the same thing each time you use it (Corcoran & Gingerich, 1992, p. 35).

The type of measure most commonly used is often referred to as *a rapid assessment instrument* (RAI). A rapid assessment instrument may be an index, a checklist, a scale, or an inventory. *Rapid* refers to the ease with which it can be completed because of its clear language, uncomplicated instructions, and brevity. RAIs are completed by the family, the practitioner, or significant others and are used to *assess* the degree, intensity, or magnitude of the problem being measured. Twenty or fewer items are considered short, but measures will vary in length and in the amount of time needed by a family or individual to complete them. Scoring is also uncomplicated and takes very little time. The results are easily interpreted using the guidelines provided with the instrument.

Using a rapid assessment instrument can (1) help evaluate the accuracy of the family assessment, (2) determine the appropriateness of the intervention plan, and (3) indicate the degree of success of the interventions used. Clinical judgments can be enhanced through systematic measurement using a standardized measure. These measures do not require adherence to a particular theoretical stance or specific intervention strategies. Flexibility in thinking is possible. The scores collected by measuring the same problem or concern at various points can easily be plotted on a graph to provide a visual representation of change, as the score obtained at one time can be compared to another. Visual accounts are powerful feedback mechanisms of change.

Rapid assessment instruments have many advantages, but it is important that you do not rely fully on these tools for the complete picture of the family or its problems. Remember that the information you receive from these measures is only an estimate, a one-time picture of the problem as measured by the instrument.

These measures rely on a small set of domains of a given problem and as such do not provide information about all dimensions of the situation. Family functioning is complex. For example, a depression scale may ask about a person's withdrawing from friends but not tap similar behavior with family or the fact that the person has few social contacts to begin with. After comparing the psychometric and practical considerations of six commonly used family functioning scales, Tutty (1995) suggested that practitioners approach measures with caution. She recommends three measures of family functioning: (1) Family Assessment Device (FAD), (2) Index of Family Relations (IFR), and (3) Self-Report Family Inventory (SFI). More specific tools are discussed in later sections of this chapter.

## Guidelines for Using Measurement Tools

Measurement is not an end in itself. It is a means by which you and family members can gain clarity about the focus of change and how you will know when change has occurred. The success or failure of measuring progress may well depend on how you present the measurement tasks to the family. The following guidelines adapted from Thomlison and Bradshaw (in press) will help you present the measure in the best possible light:

1. *Be familiar with the measure.* Gain some firsthand experience by completing the measure yourself. This way you will know how it works and how long it will take to complete. You will also become familiar with the language used in the measure. Families often ask the meaning of words or the intent of questions that we might take for granted. Do it first!

2. *Discuss with the family the importance and purpose of the measure.* Let them know what they will gain from the experience, and what information they will and will not receive from it. An open discussion is essential and alleviates anxieties and generates cooperation.

3. *Address the family with accuracy and honesty about the purpose and focus of the measure.* They may need to be convinced that an accurate snapshot is more beneficial than a flattering one. This will be easier if you have developed trust within the engagement phase of the helping relationship.

4. *Be sure the measure is culturally sensitive and gender bias free.* Review the measure with the family before they are asked to complete it on their own. Be sensitive to a number of family factors, including literacy as well as social and cultural issues that may influence the family's ability to complete the measure. You may need to make some adaptations for the administration of the measure, such as reading it to the family, making a tape recording of the measure, or substituting more appropriate language.

5. *Give feedback.* Give the family specific feedback from the measure. This means giving them more than just the total score. You can use individual items or details from the measure to discuss strengths as well as areas for further intervention and change. Measures are a form of clinical intervention, and families want to know how their problem is viewed and how it is changing. It is a form of feedback and motivation.

Remember that all measurement should be simple, practical, unobtrusive, and culturally appropriate; it should provide valuable information for you and the family.

## Measuring Common Family Problems

There are many standardized measures in the literature that can be used in assessing change and goal attainment of the family system or members of the family. An overview of a few of these measures is provided here. For a comprehensive review of the RAI literature, you may want to refer to Fischer and Corcoran (1994).

Rapid assessment instruments that can be helpful in the assessment of families include both multidimensional and specific problem indexes. These problem-oriented rapid assessment measures are helpful for tracking progress. Even though the measures focus on problems, you can use details from the instrument to highlight family strengths. While you focus on these problem areas, keep in mind the impact of other environmental systems on the functioning of the family and family members. Rapid assessment instruments developed by social worker W. W. Hudson (1992) are relevant to family and individual functioning and meet the criteria discussed earlier.

Many families will come to you with multiple problems. A multiproblem assessment instrument may be the best way to obtain an overall picture of the family's functioning during the assessment phase. An excellent example of this type of assessment instrument is the Multi-Problem Screening Inventory (MPSI) (Hudson, 1992). This instrument assesses 27 common areas of family and individual functioning, such as family relationship problems, alcohol and drug abuse, personal stress, and partner or child problems. With some families, the MPSI may be given in its entirety to identify specific problem areas. These areas may then be explored in depth with problem-specific standardized measures. With other families, one or several parts of the MPSI may be of specific relevance, and only these parts may need to be administered.

Measures that contribute to the assessment of families with multiple problems cluster around issues such as child problems, parent and/or marital problems, and family stress. A review of some rapid assessment instruments will be organized using these broad categories. The reader is referred to Corcoran and Fischer (1994) for greater detail and information about the measures.

### Family Functioning
Measures for overall family functioning, with children age 12 or above, include the following inventories.

- The Family Assessment Device (FAD) (Epstein, Baldwin, & Bishop, 1983) contains 60 items on a 4-point, Likert-type scale, measuring family problem solving, communication, roles, affective responsiveness, affective involvement, and behavior control. There is also a 12-item General Functioning Scale that can be used as a global measure of family health/pathology (Tutty, 1995).

- The Index of Family Relations (IFR) (Hudson, 1990a) is a 25-item measure, on a 5-point, Likert-type scale, requiring 10 minutes to administer. This unidimensional scale measures the severity and extent of problems experienced by family members (overall family stress—how well family members get along).
- The Self-Report Family Inventory (SFI) (Beavers & Hampson, 1990) is a 36-item measure on a 5-point, Likert-type scale, requiring 15 minutes to administer. This scale is associated with a model of healthy family functioning (Tutty, 1995) and may be useful on diverse ethnic and socioeconomic family structures.

## Child Problems

Hard-to-manage child behaviors may result in many different forms of parent-child conflict. The following measures focus on the parent-child relationship or subsystem. They measure the impact of both child and parent behaviors on the quality of this relationship. Assessing specifics of child behaviors can be done with other standardized assessment instruments, such as the Behavior Rating Index for Children (Stiffman, Orme, Evans, Feldman, & Keeney, 1984) or the Eyberg Child Behavior Inventory (Burns & Patterson, 1990).

- The Multi-Problem Screening Inventory (Hudson, 1990b) contains 13 items about the parents' perception of their relationship with the child, while other scales assess areas of functioning, such as school problems and family problems. The Index of Family Relations and the Index of Brother and Sister Relations (Hudson, 1992) measure the extent to which family members have problems in their relationships with one another.
- The Child's Attitude Toward Father and Mother Scales (Hudson, 1992) uses 25 items to assess some problems children have with their parents.
- The Parent-Child Relationship Survey (Fine & Schwebel, 1983) has 24 items that are designed to assess the quality of the parent-child relationship from the parent's point of view.

## Parent and Marital Problems

Parenting skills and parent characteristics, such as depression, marital conflict, or substance abuse, have a profound effect on the negative-feedback loop between parent and child that often develops into negative event chains within the family. Several rapid assessment instruments can measure the degree or intensity of such parent problems:

*Parenting Skills* Poor parenting skills often influence the child problems that bring families to seek help.

- The Adult-Adolescent Parenting Inventory (Bavolek, 1984) is a 32-item measure that assesses the parenting and child-rearing domains of expectations, empathy to child needs, discipline practices, and parent-child roles of both the adolescent and the parents.

- The Parental Nurturance Scale (Buri, Misukanis, & Mueller, 1994) assesses the level of parental nurturance and care from the child's perspective.
- The Parental Locus of Control Scale (Campis, Lyman, & Prentice-Dunn, 1986) is designed to assess the child versus parent power in child-rearing situations.
- The Parental Bonding Instrument (Parker, Tupling, & Brown, 1979) offers an assessment of the parental attitudes and behaviors from the child's viewpoint.

*Marital Conflict*  Marital conflict can lead to significant repercussions within the family such as family dissolution and divided loyalty.

- The Multi-Problem Screening Inventory (Hudson, 1992) contains sections on sexual discord and partner problems. The Index of Marital Satisfaction (Hudson, 1992) measures the presence and magnitude of problems in the couple relationship.
- The Kansas Marital Conflict Scale (Eggeman, Moxley, & Schumm, 1985) assesses the stages of marital conflict and the responses of both parties.
- The Beier-Sternberg Discord Questionnaire (Beier & Sternberg, 1977) assesses two domains of the couple relationship: the degree of agreement and disagreement on key couple issues and the level of unhappiness associated with any marital conflict.

*Family Violence*  Family problems can be related to partner abuse. This abuse may take many forms: emotional, financial, physical, and/or sexual abuse. The abuse may be limited to the adult partner or may also involve the children directly. Either way, any form of within-family abuse will impact the family as a whole and each member.

- The Multi-Problem Screening Inventory (Hudson, 1990a) contains 13 questions about the parents' perception of their relationship with the child—possible child maltreatment. The Partner Abuse Scale (non-physical and physical) (Hudson, 1992), as well as the Non-Physical Abuse of Partner Scale and Physical Abuse of Partner Scale (Garner & Hudson, 1992), assesses the physical and nonphysical abuse that one partner discloses having inflicted on the other partner or having received from the partner. The scales measure three types of nonphysical abuse: emotional, sexual, and financial abuse.
- The Conflict Tactics Scales (Straus & Gelles, 1990) attempt to measure three factors related to violence in the family: reasoning, verbal aggression, and physical violence.

*Child Maltreatment*  Risk assessment for child maltreatment forms an important part of some family assessments. These measures attempt to predict the harm potential for the children *within* the family setting. The instruments generally consider multiple dimensions, including child, caretaker, and family characteristics as well as environmental and parent-child interaction factors. Evaluating the likelihood of future harm to children remaining in the family is a daunting task even with the assistance of risk assessment scales. Limitations of these measures have been noted by Wald and Woolverton (1990), but many child protection agencies use them as well as others to assess family potential for reabuse. Some of the characteristics measured by the multidimensional measures include (1) child characteristics, (2) family characteristics, (3) environmental factors, (4) access to the child by the perpetrator, (5) caretaker characteristics, (6) maltreatment characteristics, and (7) parent-child interaction (Jordan & Franklin, 1995, p. 254). Three examples of risk assessment scales follow:

- The Child Well-Being Scales (Magura & Moses, 1986) measure a child's well-being in terms of which physical, social, and emotional needs are met. Used to document the severity of various forms of maltreatment in behavior-specific terms, the instrument has 43 separate factors that measure four categories: parenting role performance, familial capacities, child role performance, and child capacities from adequate to increasingly inadequate.

- The Family Risk Scales (Magura, Silverman-Moses, & Jones, 1987) measure parent characteristics and family conditions using individual rating scales to measure risk on 26 dimensions of child and caretaker characteristics. This measure looks specifically at the need for out-of-home placement and the need for and effectiveness of preventive services (Marks & McDonald, 1989).

- The Illinois CANTS (Illinois Division of Child Protection, 1985) measure identifies 13 risk factors grouped into the categories of child factors and family caretaker factors and assesses risk of both abuse and neglect. Priority assignment of cases, risk of harm to a child, and resolution of eight investigative decisions is included (Illinois Department of Social Services, 1985).

*Substance Abuse*   Substance abuse may be an important factor in family problem develop and maintenance.

- The Multi-Problem Screening Inventory (Hudson, 1990a, 1992) contains two sections related to substance abuse: alcohol abuse and drug abuse. The statements explore the extent of the problem and the impact on family members.

- The Index of Alcohol Involvement (Hudson & Garner, 1992) will measure the degree of problems related to the use of alcohol by a family member.

*Family and Environmental Stress*   Stress will have a strong influence on family problems. At times of stress, family members are often not able to access usual areas of strengths. Stress may be either chronic or more situational. The sources of stress may be related to child and/or family development events, marital stress, extended family situations, and community factors.

- The Multi-Problem Screening Inventory (Hudson, 1992) contains a section on personal stress. The Index of Clinical Stress (Hudson, 1992) measures the family's level of stress as they perceive it.

- The Impact of Events Scale (Horowitz, Wilner, & Alvarez, 1979) can be used to assess the level of stress associated with traumatic events.

- The Adolescent-Family Inventory of Life Events and Changes (McCubbin, Patterson, Bauman, & Harris, 1991) is designed to measure changes within the family by assessing changes in the level of family stress as perceived by adolescent family members.

- The Family Coping Inventory (McCubbin, Boss, Wilson, & Dahl, 1991) is a 70-item measure of partner responses to family stress.

- The Family Hardiness Index (McCubbin, McCubbin, & Thompson, 1991) is designed to assess family hardiness using 20 statements that indicate the amount of control over outcomes of life events that family members perceive they have.

## Evaluating Family Change

Although you are probably observing positive results during the treatment of the family, the best results are those that are maintained over time or continue long after you have terminated services. But remember, the goals you set with the family in the beginning provide a basis for evaluation of the intervention plan. You had a set of goals that you established in some priority order. You defined the goals clearly and identified specific objectives so you would know whether you were progressing toward the goal. This is the evaluation process. Evaluation is a systematic set of activities designed to measure either the effectiveness of the change process or the outcomes of the change efforts. Monitoring is an activity that helps to keep track of changes and considers how well these goals are being achieved. Is there progress toward the resolution of the target problem behaviors?

### Monitoring

Monitoring involves ongoing data collection to obtain new information and/or to point to the need for a change of interventions. Data are collected on family characteristics, problems, and services provided as well as on changes during treatment, at termination, and even after discharge. Continuous evaluation functions as a feedback system, informing the family about their progress and allowing the practitioner to modify and improve intervention activities if needed (Thomlison & Bradshaw, in press).

### Evaluation

A number of factors may go into your decision of how to evaluate progress. Various reasons for using practice evaluation strategies include these:

1. Evaluation assists the practitioner and the family in identifying and assessing the impact of problem areas on family functioning.

2. Evaluation provides evidence of improvement to the family and the practitioner, as well as others, such as a child's school. Regular feedback can be instrumental in helping everyone maintain an effective motivation level and commitment to the change process.

3. Ongoing evaluation will provide the practitioner with objective information to report at case conferences.

4. Agency services can be enhanced through commitment to outcome evaluation.

5. Consistent use of evaluation strategies promotes a more objective, systematic approach to the provision of services to families (Thomlison & Bradshaw, 1999).

Evaluation of practice parallels the clinical problem-solving process as follows: (1) deciding what to measure and specification of the goal, (2) determining the method of evaluation, (3) collecting and analyzing the data, and (4) sharing the knowledge gained with the family. The chosen measurements are repeated at specified points throughout the assessment, intervention, and follow-up periods. The results are recorded in such a way as to facilitate change comparisons.

Zastrow (1995) summarizes seven steps in evaluation.

1. *Specify the goal.* Goals need to be formulated in specific, concrete, and measurable terms. A specific goal should reflect the presence rather than the absence of something. Well-formulated goals will concretely state what will be different when treatment has been completed. A concrete goal is measurable and usually involves a change in *behavior* (thoughts, actions, feelings, or attitudes), a change in the *quantity and/or quality* of relationships, or a change in some aspect of the *environment,* such as a change in living arrangements or school situation.

2. *Select suitable measures.* One of the most challenging issues is determining how you will measure the change. Selecting a suitable measurement tool for the goals involves considering how you can quantify the desired outcomes. For example, has change occurred—yes or no? This would represent the most basic means of evaluating change. However, most evaluations include various levels or degrees of change. The strengths, needs, and diversity of the family system, as well as your agency requirements, must be taken into account in selecting appropriate ways of measuring. Whenever possible, choose measurement instruments that have reported reliability and validity. Examples of each of these types of measures for practitioners are readily available in social work texts (for example, see Fischer & Corcoran, 1994; Hudson, 1992; Tripodi, 1994; Zastrow, 1995).

3. *Record baseline data.* The baseline establishes the level, stability, and trend of the family's functioning prior to any specific intervention. During the assessment period, this usually requires a minimum of three data points, or until a stable data pattern is obtained. This becomes the standard against which any changes accompanying the intervention can be evaluated. If the family system is in crisis or danger, immediate intervention is essential. In such circumstances, the social worker would proceed with intervention and repeatedly measure the family's progress during the treatment phase.

4. *Implement intervention and continue monitoring.* At specified intervals, such as every month or every week, the same measurement tool would be given as for the baseline. This provides information on whether progress is being made and can be valuable information for deciding whether change strategies or objectives need to be revised.

5. *Assess change.* Creating a chart or graph from the data collected facilitates a visual analysis of your measurements. This visual representation of change can provide important information to both you and the family on whether change is in the desired direction.

6. *Infer effectiveness.* Making an inference about whether your intervention was responsible for family outcomes involves determining whether there could be other explanations for the change. Possible sources for change besides your interventions include history (events that occurred during the time of treatment but were not related to the treatment); maturation (the effects of time); multiple-treatment interference (more than one treatment received); and statistical regression (high and low scores on measures tend to move toward the mean or average score when retested) (Zastrow, 1995). All of these factors make it difficult to know exactly whether the change is the result of the intervention.

7. *Follow up.* It is important to assess the maintenance and generalization of change by contacting the family at a three-month and six-month interval after termination. "The purposes of follow-up are to determine whether the positive changes during intervention persist on removal of the intervention, the problem recurs or relapses, new problems appear, and/or the social worker should reinstitute intervention" (Tripodi, 1994, p. 86). If maintenance of the change is an issue, activities include stabilizing success, firming up social supports, and transitioning to the future (Ivanoff & Stern, 1992; Zastrow, 1995).

Achievements need to be integrated into the daily functioning of families for maximum stabilization of success. This is best accomplished throughout the treatment process where emphasis is placed on practicing learned skills and behaviors. This type of behavior change will promote family self-confidence. Reviewing their successes and strengths helps families feel more confident about approaching related issues in the future. Support networks apart from formal social services are important for maintaining changes accomplished during the intervention phases.

Incorporating evaluation into the intervention process requires deciding who will measure what, when, and how the information will be shared. Deciding what to measure is primarily grounded in what the family considers important, for example:

- Change in circumstances, such as separation, move of child from home
- Change in attitude, such as increased self-respect and family identity
- Change in skills, such as increased parenting skills
- Change in behavior, such as increased time spent with parents, increased life satisfaction

It is important to remember that measurement is not an end in itself but an important way in which you and the family can gain clarity about the focus of change and how both of you will know when change has occurred. The success or failure of measurement depends on how you present the measurement task to the family.

# Summary of Practice Principles

1. Social workers and practitioners use a combination of practical and empirical strategies for evaluating family change. Fischer and Corcoran (1994) have compiled a list of measures for adults, children, and couples to assess a number of psychological, behavioral, and interpersonal difficulties. The measures have been reproduced, and you can examine them to find one suitable for clinical practice.

2. There are several guidelines that you should follow before using any type of measurement method in your practice. Remember, all measurement needs to be simple, practical, unobtrusive, culturally appropriate, and of importance to client and social worker.

3. In summary:
   - Start with the question, What information is needed?
   - Choose goals (outcomes) that are simple, practical, and meaningful for the family.
   - Measure one or two things well.
   - Involve the family in defining the outcomes to measure.
   - Review and revise the measure with the family who will be using it.
   - Build on what the family is prepared to document.
   - Measure often.

# Learning Activities

## Activity 6.1: Evaluate yourself

Look for a standardized assessment instrument (Fischer & Corcoran, 1994) and complete an assessment on yourself.

1. Write an assessment and treatment plan based on the results of that one test.
2. Are the scores you obtained similar to your professional judgment about the most relevant problems you face?
3. If you were providing services to a family, what would be your initial point of focus in the introduction of an assessment measure?
4. What were your experiences in conducting an assessment on yourself? Were you uncomfortable? How would you deal with these feelings in families?
5. Now, administer the same measure or a different one on a colleague. Practice introducing the measure and scoring and interpreting the results. Give the results orally to your colleague.

# PART TWO

# Self-Assessment and Critical Thinking

▼▼▼

# CHAPTER SEVEN

# *Examining Your Own Family Experience*

*Write down everything, leave nothing standing. Experiences, meanings, theories, and concepts. All are relevant? . . . I've learned about personal views on health and families to a great extent. In many cases, I've discovered insights and meaning I never knew I had. The journaling really has been beneficial. It's encouraged me to explore my beliefs, examine them for meanings, and question the origin of these values.*

*Student*

Part II of this book is quite different from Part I. In this chapter, the focus is on application of family systems, learning to your own family life experiences. It is focused on learning about you and understanding about you within the context of your family. Writing about your family forms a different kind of context for learning. Learning also comes through your experiences and applying theory to these. Through assessing your family system and critically reflecting on your own events and situations, you also learn about families. You will learn several things:

1. To integrate family content knowledge with life experiences to assist in your understanding of family dynamics.
2. To examine the process of a family—your own—in order to understand the family as a constantly changing system influencing belief systems, behaviors, and relationships.
3. To build on what you bring from your family experiences, to personalize your approach to practice and learning, and to understand the diversity of ideas and outcomes when applying the family assessment process to practice.

A picture is worth a thousand words, and a good example is even better. Learning about families requires moving from what you know to more detailed challenges and requirements for greater depth of knowledge. Focusing on your own family teaches you to be more sensitive to the diverse family processes and outcomes that you will encounter in practice. Self-assessment and critical thinking about your family system can illustrate clearly how and why the family assessment process is a dynamic entity of multiple processes. It also can show you that to reach new heights in understanding a family requires you to seek new levels of understanding about your own family.

Because critical thinking is often defined in many ways, clarification of this concept is important. While it is often defined as a questioning approach to issues, a broader meaning is more useful to practitioners, such as the one used by Paul and Binker (1990): "The art of thinking about your thinking while you are thinking in order to make your thinking better; more clear, more accurate, or more defensible" (p. 643).

This chapter is a major assignment to be completed throughout the family course and is a supplement to the various topics in family assessment and interventions. It is intended to provoke you into examining yourself and reflecting on how the values, beliefs, rules, rituals, and traditions of your own family shaped your behavior and thinking in adulthood. Personal views and stories shape the way we see and experience others. Moreover, our family belief systems influence our interactions with other families and can be a source of bias in our practice. It is hoped that by examining these family influences you will learn from this critical thinking process and thereby be in a better position to understand other families. To gain the most understanding from this chapter, you must be honest about yourself and your family life. Keeping a family journal is one of the best ways for you to discover your own family influences.

## *Journal Writing*

The journal, or directed diary, is a writing tool for learning about you. It can be simple or complicated. Above all, it is a tool for critical thinking. The journal is an ancient tool that goes back to the 10th century, when Japanese ladies of the court used their "pillow book" to reflect on life and love. During the 17th century, Protestants and Puritans applauded the self-discipline of diary keeping. As a student, you should find that journal writing will help you recount events and thoughts about growing up in your family. You can retrace the subjective, lived meaning (Reimer, Thomlison, & Bradshaw, 1999, p. 140).

Journaling is somewhat different from keeping a diary. Writing to the journal questions, you will primarily focus on external and internal events and structures influencing you and your family. Through self-examination and reflection, you will find that journal writing is a safe place to raise issues, deal with your fears and concerns, and come to understand how these events and family stories shaped the adult person you became.

Journal writing is a useful analytical tool. The purpose of recounting through writing what happened in the family is to focus or reflect on the significance of activities or events as they relate to learning to work with families. Although recounting significant and meaningful events is important, it is the process of writing and reflecting on those events and understanding differently now as an adult that is most meaningful. Through directed journal questions, areas of family life are reviewed in an effort to construct and deconstruct information to help you understand how families are formed and what maintains their dynamics. It also helps us to understand rights and responsibilities of families, uniqueness and differentness in families, and ways our values are formed. Through the process of thinking critically by journal writings, you can search for details of events, patterns, and themes, all of which impact self-awareness. The classic analytical framework of "who, why, when, where, what, and how" are always useful in reaching conclusions about what you are learning about your family. In turn, this will be relevant to your learning needs.

## Critical Thinking and Self-Assessment

The secret to writing about your family is simply to start. What does matter is that you begin to put your thoughts, ideas, and feelings on paper in response to the assigned questions. It is a purposeful process designed to clarify thinking and to form a baseline against which you are able to measure changes in yourself. For example, are you comfortable with your communication skills with families? Do you feel anxious when you raise parent-child conflicts? Do you feel uncomfortable approaching women about family finances? Are you proud of your relationship skills with adolescents? These feelings and thoughts may be related to your own family experiences and, therefore, you need to become aware of this relationship so that it won't influence your work with families. Each time you write you engage in appraising your thinking. You will want to review your responses for themes, ideas, and patterns. As well, you will need to consider what the events meant and how you felt about them. Journaling is a way of organizing and summarizing thoughts. Reread your entries aloud as a form of feedback (Reimer, Thomlison, & Bradshaw, 1999, p. 140).

## What Will I Learn?

As a student, you will discover that journal writing involves much more than the writing and appraisal of thoughts and events in your family's life. Journaling involves the careful examination and evaluation of beliefs, feelings, and actions. Well-reasoned thinking is a creative form of understanding your purpose and learning about you.

The purposes of journaling are self-assessment and self-improvement. Through journal writing you will discover assumptions, alternative explanations, and biases about yourself as a developing professional. You will also discover your abilities and strengths. From this self-discovery process you will uncover thinking and learning styles, attitudes, and strategies associated with yourself as a developing professional. Self-assessment is viewed as an opportunity for learning. Each time you engage in appraising your thinking you are also helping your families in valuable ways. It will help you plan for safe, high-quality decisions and options for family services.

Some guidelines for analyzing and thinking critically about your responses to the family questions include these:

- Thinking in terms of opposites
- Exploring feelings by exploring different views from different perspectives
- Focusing on problem finding and problem solving

- Emphasizing understanding
- Questioning practices, rules, thinking about family life
- Reflecting on experiences
- Recognizing the affective or emotional influences
- Recognizing attitudes and values associated with cognitive biases
- Reflecting on self-awareness by asking, What do I believe? Why do I believe that?
- Identifying recurrent patterns of interaction
- Differentiating fact from opinion
- Connecting with your current beliefs and thinking (Reimer, Thomlison, Bradshaw, 1999, p. 141)

Now that you understand the purpose of looking at your family you are ready to begin to explore ideas, beliefs, and attitudes about content and process from the following questions. Accomplishing this task requires you to be both honest and willing to write your "stories" with integrity. Remember, write respecting confidentiality within your own family constellation.

Writing is a learning tool for heightening and refining the process of reflection. The purpose of writing about the events and experiences from your family is to reflect or think about their meaning for you as a student learner and developing professional. The more you become aware of the significance of these developing experiences, the more you are able to tap into your inner strengths and capacities. The focus will be on your unfolding awareness of self and the meaning, values, and interrelationships you are discovering in your analysis. Reflection promotes inner or emotional awareness. It is a cognition process. In fact, putting pen to paper or fingers to laptop is what compels us to reflect rather than ruminate. Reflecting on your writing enables you to draw on inherent resources. Journal writing is then able to generate positive thoughts and provide you with a clearer sense of self. These entries will help you use your strengths in improving your practice.

# My Family Journal

## Activity 7.1: Life Summary

Complete the life summary profile. Various life summaries are used in adoption and child welfare settings.

1. Birth Information (as much as possible for weight, time, date, and name as spelled out on birth certificate)

_____

_____

_____

_____

_____

2. Biological Parents

_____

_____

_____

_____

Physical descriptions

_____

_____

_____

_____

_____

_____

Descriptions of personal qualities

_____

_____

_____

_____

_____

_____

Current

_____
_____
_____
_____
_____
_____

Any key information about the parents that is notable

_____
_____
_____
_____
_____

Any messages from parents that you may remember

_____
_____
_____
_____
_____

3. Other Family of Origin Information

Sibling information, names, birthdates

_____
_____
_____
_____
_____
_____

Your relationship with siblings and their whereabouts

_____
_____
_____
_____
_____
_____

Other significant family members, including grandparents, aunts, uncles, and cousins

_____

_____

_____

_____

_____

_____

_____

4. Residence and Location History—Did your family move? List in chronological order: dates, locations, address, reason for move, etc.

_____

_____

_____

_____

_____

_____

_____

_____

_____

5. Attachments—Relational History

Identify any significant relationships in childhood—adults, friends, teachers, pets, etc.

_____

_____

_____

_____

_____

_____

_____

_____

_____

_____

_____

6. Social and Emotional Competencies as a Child

How you were described as a child—attitude, behaviors, talents, abilities, etc.

_____
_____
_____
_____
_____
_____
_____

Activities you were involved in as a child

_____
_____
_____
_____
_____
_____
_____

Achievements or special moments

_____
_____
_____
_____
_____
_____
_____

Problems?

_____
_____
_____
_____
_____
_____

7. School and Learning History

    All information on schools, classroom placements, and progress; abilities and difficulties; any teachers' comments remembered; and interests and involvement

    _____

    _____

    _____

    _____

    _____

    _____

    _____

8. Health and Development History

    Birth problems, medical problems or concerns, hospitalizations, family of origin health problems

    _____

    _____

    _____

    _____

    _____

    _____

    _____

9. Significant Events and Self-Perceptions from Childhood

    _____

    _____

    _____

    _____

    _____

    _____

    _____

10. Pictures

    Include a picture of yourself as a child.

## Activity 7.2: Family Development

1. The Family System

   Using your family once again, analyze the family from a multisystemic perspective. Appraise the family system and its functioning. What intervention do you think is warranted to address family issues? Describe the intervention.

2. Family of Origin and Roles

   Assess your family system and family culture. Draw a three-generation family genogram. To understand the role of uniqueness and culture in the formation and development of the family system, place cultural symbols on the genogram. Mark your genogram with appropriate data and symbols using a legend. Colors can be used. To be included with your genogram, write a portion of an assessment report about the family structure, development, and culture. Here are some questions to consider:

   a. Describe the family of origin, including information on family structure, cultural identity, racial and ethnic background, special affiliations, sociocultural characteristics, the neighborhood, and other factors you feel are important to understanding your family as presented.

   b. How have the above factors influenced the family? What is the impact of these historical factors on the family now, including issues of discrimination, current issues of concern, issues of similarities and differences that contributed to the family's uniqueness?

   c. What are some of the things you learned about the historical context of the family, about people who are different from the racial, ethnic, or sexual orientation of the family; the roles of women and men; the place of children? Who is defined as an outsider or insider, and how are they treated?

   d. Identify some of the biases, prejudices, and stereotypes you learned from your family of origin.

3. Social Network Map and Grid

   Assess your family system and its social network map. Draw a family social network map and complete the social network grid (Chapter 4). Write a summary narrative of the social network map and system of your family.

4. Family Rules, Rituals, and Traditions

   a. Identify rituals and traditions that exist in your family. Why do they exist?

   b. Identify a transition that would be appropriate for a ritual.

   c. Using the information in your journal, construct a new ritual for your family. Be sure to incorporate the developmental level of family members, the life cycle stage, the purpose, etc.

   d. Identify which occasions should be marked in families. How do you mark these in your family?

   e. How would you assist a family in developing rituals and traditions?

   f. Identify a family transition issue and the likely impact on your family.

g. Develop a plan to assist the family to deal with this transition.

h. How would your family be different without rituals and traditions?

5. Family Connections

Family development, connections, and family patterns are relationships that are maintained across generations in families. Thinking about your family, examine the relationships and family patterns that are significant in your life.

a. Who in your family had a strong influence on your development?

b. How did you feel about being cared for by people other than your parents?

c. What was your relationship with extended family members?

d. What part did your grandparents, aunts, uncles, cousins, and family friends play in your life?

e. What form of discipline was used in your family most often?

f. Was the discipline the same for girls and boys?

g. What rules/expectations applied to boys and girls?

h. Who participated in the decision-making process?

i. Who did your family turn to for help when support was needed?

j. Who in the family did you turn to for help? Who helped you to solve problems?

k. What types of rewards were given for family and individual successes?

l. Describe what you hope may be the same or different in your future family compared to your family of origin.

6. Family External Systems

a. What kinds of environmental strengths and resources does your family currently use?

b. What is the nature of the relationship between your family and the external systems?

c. What strengths and resources in the environment are underutilized and could be mobilized?

d. What obstacles (internal and external to the family) prevent access to environmental resources?

e. What does your family understand about the environment?

f. What resources are needed or required that are lacking in the environment?

g. Identify your family strengths.

7. The Family Assessment Report

Complete a family assessment report following the suggestions in Chapter 5.

8. Lessons Learned

Identify 10 lessons learned from your family experience that can be guidelines for your practice with families.

# PART THREE

# Practicing Family Assessment: Case Studies

▼▼▼

# CHAPTER EIGHT

# The Sherman Family: Applying for Adoption

This case example is an assessment of the Sherman family, who wish to adopt a child. Two elements are missing: a genogram and a social network map and grid. Complete a three-generation genogram and a social network map for this family.

## Home Assessment Report for Private Adoption: The Sherman Family

### Part 1. Identifying Information and Personal History

Robert and Angela Sherman are a Caucasian American couple who hope to adopt a child. The couple met in 1984, shortly after Angela was divorced from her first husband, and they married in 1988, soon after Angela graduated from college. The following assessment information is the result of interviews at their home. Figure 8.1 is a guide for collecting the pre-adoption assessment data.

**Robert Sherman**

*Identifying Information*   Mr. Sherman, age 32 years, is 6′ tall, weighs 160 pounds, and is of medium build. He has blue eyes, brown hair, and a dark complexion. Mr. Sherman was born and raised in Cleveland, Ohio.

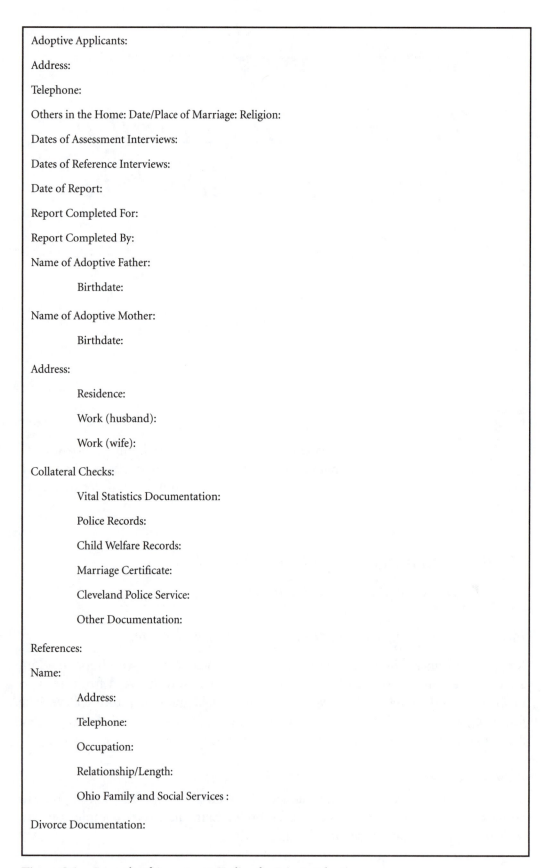

Adoptive Applicants:

Address:

Telephone:

Others in the Home: Date/Place of Marriage: Religion:

Dates of Assessment Interviews:

Dates of Reference Interviews:

Date of Report:

Report Completed For:

Report Completed By:

Name of Adoptive Father:

      Birthdate:

Name of Adoptive Mother:

      Birthdate:

Address:

      Residence:

      Work (husband):

      Work (wife):

Collateral Checks:

      Vital Statistics Documentation:

      Police Records:

      Child Welfare Records:

      Marriage Certificate:

      Cleveland Police Service:

      Other Documentation:

References:

Name:

      Address:

      Telephone:

      Occupation:

      Relationship/Length:

      Ohio Family and Social Services :

Divorce Documentation:

**Figure 8.1**    Example of Assessment Outline for Private Adoption

*Family Background/History*   Mr. Sherman is Caucasian of German descent. He is the younger of two children born to Sue and Sonny Sherman. In 1976, Sue died at the age of 38 from complications of an ulcer. Mr. Sherman was eight years old at the time. Sonny Sherman died of cancer in July 1988 at the age of 73. He had been a successful small businessman while raising his children. Mr. Sherman and his father were very close. Mr. Sherman has one older brother, Bill, who lives in Cleveland with his wife and two children. They maintain weekly contact and share a close relationship. Bill, the brother, is also an electrician and holds a supervisory position in a service company.

Mr. Sherman describes his childhood as both difficult and rewarding. Following his mother's death, he began to take on increasing amounts of responsibility for himself and for household tasks. His older brother was in his adolescence and was not as actively involved in daily tasks as was Mr. Sherman. Their father worked long hours, and Mr. Sherman became responsible for cooking, cleaning, grocery shopping, and looking after the family pet. In some ways, it was like a partnership with his father. As a result of this shared family responsibility, Mr. Sherman and his father became very good friends, as well as a close father and son. They spent a great deal of their free time on mutual interests, such as restoring antique boats. These mutual interests and shared time continued to his father's death.

From his father, Mr. Sherman learned to value independence, hard work, and the importance of family. He has worked hard for everything he has achieved in his life and feels that this is an important part of what children should learn in families. He values education and places importance on open communication in relationships. Mr. Sherman does not recall that he was ever spanked as a child. Rather, his father would spend time with him discussing the inappropriate behavior and more appropriate alternatives.

Mr. Sherman would like to raise his children in the same manner that he was raised. A major difference would be that his children would not need to take on the same degree of responsibility that he did at such an early age. Mr. Sherman was raised a Roman Catholic and attended Catholic schools while growing up. He continues to see religion as an important part of his life and would raise a child as a Christian. However, as he and his wife are of different faiths, they have not yet made a final decision on what faith the child would be raised in or if the child would have a dual religious upbringing. Mr. Sherman's brother is aware of and supportive of Mr. Sherman's desire to adopt a child.

*Education and Employment*   Mr. Sherman graduated from high school in Cleveland in 1986. He attended the Ohio Institution of Technology from 1986 to 1991 completing his training as an electrician. Following graduation he worked for Sharpe & Sharpe from 1991 to 1998. The last four years he worked for Sharpe & Sharpe were in Cleveland, Ohio, where he had moved in 1988. In 2000, Mr. Sherman moved to his present position with Trans-Cleveland Electricians as a senior electrician. Mr. Sherman indicates that he enjoys his present position and finds it both challenging and stimulating. His career goals include obtaining a managerial position, and he continues to pursue this objective. Mr. Sherman works long hours but enjoys his time off for family and personal interests.

*Health and Lifestyle*   Mr. Sherman reports that he is in excellent health. He experienced all the usual childhood ailments. He was hospitalized for the removal of a kidney stone in 1996. He has never had any mental health concerns and presents as an emotionally stable individual.

Mr. Sherman maintains a healthy lifestyle through regular exercise, not smoking, and drinking only on occasion. The use of nonprescription drugs has never been a part of his lifestyle. Mr. Sherman has no criminal record, and physical violence is unacceptable to him.

*Personal Qualities*   Mr. Sherman presents as a mature, intelligent, and dependable man with a charming sense of humor. He describes himself as friendly and caring and feels his best qualities are his ability to get along with anyone and his intelligence. His spouse describes him as loving, witty, artistic, compassionate, fun to be with, sensitive, and a good friend. She appreciates most his encouraging and supportive manner. Mr. Sherman identifies work as being stressful to some degree, but he deals with stress by relying on the support systems he has established—for example, his spouse, family, and friends—and by leaving work problems at work. He finds that he needs to have time away from work to maximize his ability to manage the ongoing stress of his job.

Mr. Sherman also has a wide range of interests and activities that he enjoys in his leisure time, including restoring antique autos, bike riding, watching movies, and spending time with his dog.

### Angela Sherman

*Identifying Information*   Angela Sherman, age 33 years, is 5′6″ tall and weighs 159 pounds. She has blue eyes, dark red hair, and a fair complexion. Mrs. Sherman was born in Charlotte, North Carolina. She moved to Cincinnati, Ohio, when she was nine years old, and approximately three years later her family moved to Cleveland, Ohio.

*Family Background/History*   Mrs. Sherman is of German and Irish descent. She is the second of three children born to Sid and Margaret Porter. Sid, age 67 years, is a retired manager for a large oil company. Margaret, age 67, was an executive before becoming a homemaker. She continues to be active in volunteer work. Mr. and Mrs. Porter have been married approximately 43 years. Mrs. Sherman describes her parents' marriage as very strong. Her parents continue to be active in their church and their community, and they are enjoying extensive traveling. As her parents now live in North Carolina, Mrs. Sherman does not see them as much as she would like. She does, however, visit with them approximately three times per year. Between visits she talks with them by telephone every other week.

Mrs. Sherman's older brother, George, age 37, is married with two children and living in North Carolina. He is employed as a manager. Mrs. Sherman's younger sister, Judy, age 29, lives in North Carolina with her husband and two small children. She is employed part-time as a technician. Mrs. Sherman indicates that she is close to her siblings and sees them when she goes home to visit with her parents.

Mrs. Sherman describes her family as loving and affectionate. They placed a focus on shared activities and she recalls time spent on family vacations and camping trips, playing games and putting puzzles together. She does not recall that she was ever physically punished as a child. Rather, her parents talked to their children about expectations regarding behavior, and if there was a problem, time was spent problem solving. Mrs. Sherman indicates that her family experienced no major difficulties as she was growing up.

Mrs. Sherman's family is very active in the Baptist church. Mrs. Sherman was involved in church youth groups and she continues to attend church services. As Mr. Sherman is of a different religion, they alternate between attending his and her religious services. Both feel strongly about the importance of raising a child with Christian beliefs, and they do not anticipate a difficulty in deciding on the child's Christian education.

From her family, Mrs. Sherman learned to value her religious beliefs, her family, and education. She would like to raise her children as she was raised. She would also encourage open communication with her children as she feels that with all the difficulties facing children and adolescents in today's society, good communication is more essential than ever.

Mrs. Sherman's family is aware and supportive of her desire to adopt. Mrs. Sherman indicates that six of her cousins are adopted and that within her extended family, adoption is viewed as a natural and loving way of forming your family.

*Education and Employment*   Mrs. Sherman graduated from high school in 1981. She was a university student from 1983 to 1987 and obtained her bachelor of education degree with a major in early childhood services. Mrs. Sherman paid for her education by working. On graduation, she had accumulated a great deal of experience in the area and found employment with an excellent company. She enjoys her work and finds it to be challenging. As her work is important to her, she is unsure exactly what she will do following an adoption. She feels it is likely that after a maternity leave she will continue at least part-time in some type of work. No plans have been made as to the exact type of child care the family would use, although options such as day care, day homes, and a nanny have been discussed.

*Health and Lifestyle*   Mrs. Sherman reports that she is in excellent health. She has had all the usual childhood diseases. Mrs. Sherman's commitment to good health is reflected in her lifestyle. She is a nonsmoker and occasional drinker. The use of nonprescription drugs has never been a part of her lifestyle. Mrs. Sherman has never been in trouble with the law, and physical violence is unacceptable to her.

*Personal Qualities*   Mrs. Sherman presents as a friendly, competent, and caring individual. She describes herself as enthusiastic, loving, compassionate, and sympathetic. She feels that one of her strongest points is her caring for others. Her spouse describes her as sensitive and fun. He feels she is his best friend. Mrs. Sherman has found her infertility to be a source of stress to her in the last several years. She copes with this stress by talking to her husband, her family, and her wide circle of friends. She finds that talking about her concerns is a very important part of how she deals with difficulties in her life. She also has a variety of interests including sewing, all types of crafts, golfing, art, home decorating, traveling, walking, and bike riding.

## Part 2. Family Dynamics and Community Relationships

*Previous Marital Relationship*   Mrs. Sherman was married prior to her present relationship. She knew her first husband for two years prior to marrying him in 1982. She did not feel that the relationship was bad or unhealthy in any way and was surprised when, without notice, her husband left the marriage. They were separated in 1984 and received their final divorce decree in the same year. In retrospect, Mrs. Sherman suspects that her husband might have been having an extramarital affair, as he married a co-worker shortly after the divorce was final. Having had one unsuccessful marriage, Mrs. Sherman feels it is very important in a relationship to have open communication about both thoughts and feelings. She indicates that she has been able to adequately resolve her feelings about the failure of her first marriage but that resolution would have been easier had she been aware of the reasons for her husband's leaving the marriage.

*Present Marital Relationship*   Mr. and Mrs. Sherman met at a company party in 1984. Two weeks after meeting, Mr. Sherman was transferred to Cleveland Shores. Mr. and Mrs. Sherman dated long-distance for four years before Mr. Sherman was able to find employment in Cleveland and move back in 1988. They both knew early in the relationship that it was serious, and this motivated their almost weekly visits with each other. After Mr. Sherman moved back to Cleveland in June, the couple were married in October of the same year.

Mr. and Mrs. Sherman describe their marriage as a loving and supportive relationship. They feel that they are similar in that they are careful, thoughtful, and analytical people. This similarity has helped them when they are attempting to work through a problem situation as they can be objective in looking at all possible problems and solutions. They make their choices based on all the information available to them at the time. When dealing with conflict in their relationship, Mr. and Mrs. Sherman attempt to acknowledge differences, communicate how they feel about the issue, and make a choice in which the individual needs of both are taken into consideration. Mrs. Sherman indicates that Mr. Sherman is not always forthcoming with his feelings and she attempts to give him an opportunity to think through what is bothering him while trying to offer him opportunities to communicate his worries to her. Thus far, this approach has met with some success and they continue to work on strengthening and improving their already strong commitment to each other.

Mr. and Mrs. Sherman also share beliefs on child rearing. They would like their children to develop a respect for themselves and others, to have Christian morals and values, to share their parents' value of family, and to understand the importance of striving to achieve their goals. Neither Mr. nor Mrs. Sherman believes that physical punishment is really necessary to discipline a child. They cannot anticipate exactly how they might react as parents but believe that nonpunitive methods of discipline would be more likely options for them.

Mr. and Mrs. Sherman have a wide and varied support network. As they are very close to Mrs. Sherman's family and Mr. Sherman's brother, they maintain regular contact with them.

They have a wide circle of friends and Mrs. Sherman also has a number of work-related friendships on which she relies for support. The Shermans believe that traditions and rituals have a role in the family and invite their family and friends to join them in their traditions. Christmas is an especially important time for this couple and they look forward to sharing it with children.

Mr. and Mrs. Sherman foster a child in a third-world country through Foster Parents of Canada. They believe it is important to assist others who have not been as fortunate as they have. They see themselves as becoming more active in their local community when they have children who become involved. They believe that it may be helpful to seek the support of other adoptive parents at some point in time to help them deal effectively with issues common to adopted children and adoptive parents. They see the Adoptive Parents Association as an appropriate agency for these types of issues. They feel comfortable seeking professional assistance with problems that they are unable to resolve on their own.

## Part 3. Home and Neighborhood

Mr. and Mrs. Sherman moved into their new home in December of 1988. It is a 2,254 square foot, two-story home. There are three bedrooms upstairs and a den on the main floor; they are completing a large recreational area in the basement. The Shermans' home is warm, welcoming, and beautifully decorated. Schools, parks, and recreational facilities are all in close proximity.

## Part 4. Income

This couple is confident in their ability to meet the financial needs of a child and to provide a financially secure home for their family. Mr. Sherman's gross annual income is $63,648.00 and his net monthly income is $3,400.00. Mrs. Sherman's gross annual income is $61,620.00 and her net monthly income is $3,492.00. They both have benefits packages through their work.

This couple's assets include $37,000.00 in savings, a $250,000.00 home, $75,000.00 in automobiles, $40,000.00 in real estate equity, and $44,000.00 in retirement savings plans.

Their monthly expenses are estimated at $1,898.00 including food, clothing, utilities, property taxes, transportation, and entertainment costs. Although they own their home, they do have another investment property on which they have a mortgage of $154,500.00. The monthly payment of $1,758.00 is covered by the renter.

Financial decision making and responsibility are shared by Mr. and Mrs. Sherman. They share similar goals and values in this area of their lives and feel able to more than adequately meet the financial responsibilities of children.

## Part 5. Understanding of Adoption and Motivation

Mrs. Sherman became aware that she might have fertility difficulties during her first marriage. In 1983 she was referred to a specialist for an introductory consultation. As her marriage ended shortly after that, she did not pursue the matter. Mr. and Mrs. Sherman began trying to conceive immediately after their marriage and were referred to an infertility clinic in March 1989. In August 1989, a laparoscopy was done on Mrs. Sherman and it was determined that she had no apparent problems except for endometriosis, which does not necessarily result in infertility. In January 1991, Mrs. Sherman had surgery for the endometriosis. Both she and her husband hope that the surgery may result in a pregnancy. However, they consider adoption as a way of building their family if they continue to be unable to conceive. As a result of this ongoing uncertainty Mr. and Mrs. Sherman have not completely resolved their feelings about their possible infertility. If they continue to be unable to conceive following the surgery, they feel that they will need to deal with and accept their infertility. They are very motivated to become parents and if unable to do so through pregnancy would very much like to adopt a child.

Mr. and Mrs. Sherman first began discussing adoption in 1988. They registered with an adoption agency in November 1990. As Mrs. Sherman has so many adopted cousins, she is very comfortable with the idea of adoption. The Shermans feel that adoption should be an open issue and that children should be told from the time they are very small that they are adopted. The Shermans feel sure that adoptees will go through periods of wondering about their birthparents and that parents can be helpful by being honest and giving them any age-appropriate information they may want.

Mr. and Mrs. Sherman express great empathy for the birth mother and the difficult decision she has to make for her child. They would be comfortable with meeting the birth parents prior to placement and would accept letters, photographs, and gifts from the birth parents for their child. The Shermans would not be comfortable with ongoing contact following placement.

Mr. and Mrs. Sherman attended a workshop for adoptive couples in November 1990 and show a good understanding of the issues specific to parenting an adopted child. They both feel strongly that is important to treat children with love and respect and to deal with any issues about adoption with openness and honesty. They feel that the challenges associated with parenting an adopted child would be worth undertaking, considering the rewards of parenting.

## Part 6. Child Desired

Mr. and Mrs. Sherman would like to adopt a healthy Caucasian infant of either sex. They would consider a child of up to six months of age and would be open to twins. They are not open to a child conceived by rape or incest. They would prefer to have information on the background of both birth parents. They would have concerns if there was a history of mental illness, learning disabilities, mental retardation, a criminal history, history of drug use, prostitution, and some history of smoking and drinking in the background of either birth parent. They would consider a child born with a minor repairable birth defect but would not be willing to accept a child with an obvious physical defect or handicap.

## Part 7. References

All references were interviewed and support was given to Mr. and Mrs. Sherman's application to adopt a child. This couple was described as honest, hardworking, and loving; they were seen to value family relationships highly. They have the desire to parent and the ability to manage the challenge of parenting an adopted child. The references felt that the Shermans share a relationship based on mutual respect, caring, and shared interests and values. All the references stated that they would be comfortable leaving their children in the care of Mr. and Mrs. Sherman, knowing they would be well cared for. Overall, the couple were seen as being highly motivated to parent and well able to meet, and to share together, the social, emotional, physical, and intellectual needs of a child placed in their care.

## Part 8. Overview of Assessment Process

Mr. and Mrs. Sherman were interviewed in their home on December 1 and December 2, 1999. Prior to their home assessment, the couple had given the issue of adding to their family through adoption considerable thought and had discussed their hopes of adopting with others in their support network. In November 1990, they registered with a private adoption agency and attended a pre-adoption workshop for adoptive parents.

## Part 9. Summary

Mr. and Mrs. Sherman present as a mature couple whose marriage is marked by caring, support, and respect. This couple is sincere in their desire to parent and if unable to conceive would like to build their family through adoption. They have given the issues of adoption serious consideration. They display comfort with the process of open adoption and it is believed they will manage the challenges of adoption with success.

Mr. and Mrs. Sherman are realistic about the responsibilities of parenting an adopted child. They are able to provide a secure and loving home for a child. They have a strong support network to whom they turn easily for advice and support.

## Part 10. Recommendation

It is recommended that Mr. and Mrs. Sherman be approved as candidates for the private adoption of a child.

Respectfully submitted,


Debbie Cattrello, M.S.W.
Adoption Worker

▼▼▼

# CHAPTER NINE

# The Del Sol Family: Marital Conflict and Parenting Concerns

The case study of the Del Sol family provides opportunities for you to learn about assessing a family as well as to practice and discuss family assessment. Study questions and exercises may be done independently as a form of self-study or in peer group learning situations. Some exercises are more relevant than others to the work of particular individuals and groups. Remember that different and creative responses are acceptable as you plan interventions. The basis of this case is from my practice/research, but it is essentially a composite of child and family situations.

## Study Activities

Not all items will apply to the case, but all included here are to stimulate your thinking about family assessment and intervention.

1. What are the family issues?
2. What are the family and individual needs for
   - Concrete, instrumental support?
   - Information, knowledge, and skills?
   - Emotional supports?
   - Affiliational supports?

3. Analyze the family system:

   a. Examine the family member boundaries—a critical task in determining family interaction patterns, roles and power, and parenting issues. Describe the boundaries, interaction patterns, roles and power, and parenting issues in the case.

   b. Describe the situation in the family regarding

      - Emotional connections.
      - Resources within the family.

   c  Describe what a family-centered approach will look like in this family.

   d. Answer the following questions about the family unit in this case:

      - What systems are apparent at the individual and family level?
      - What functions are performed by which family systems and how well do the systems function?
      - Do any boundaries need to be changed? What needs to be done? Describe how you will do this.
      - What are the family system strengths and problems?
      - Family behaviors are best understood from a circular causality rather than a linear causality. Using an example from this case, where might you use a circular perspective to make a cognitive change, affective change, or behavioral change?
      - What are examples of risk factors in this case?
      - What are examples of strengths in this case?
      - What stage of development is the family in?
      - What are the tasks associated with this stage of development?
      - What are the stressors associated with the tasks?
      - How have the stressors impacted family development?
      - What events have impacted the family structure and family membership at this stage?

4. *Family Assessment:* The goal of this activity is to document and develop knowledge of the culture of the Del Sol family. Several tasks are required and approximately two hours will be needed to complete this group activity, which starts with a role play of a family interview. The class can be divided into small groups, each engaging in a family interview role play; another option is for one small group to role-play, with other classmates observing and recording, followed by large group discussion. Be sure to have a flip chart available to document or illustrate the cultural genogram or social network map, and have a copy of the social network grid for this interview.

   a. Students should assume the roles of the Del Sol family members (Rosa, mother; Miguel, father; nine-year-old Christopher, stepson) and an interviewer.

   b. This is the first interview with the Del Sol family, and the focus of the family meeting is on obtaining information related to the family's culture and history. Questions to consider for the cultural assessment follow:

- Where did the family come from?
- When did they come to this country?
- What were the circumstances that brought them to this country?
- What is important to this family?
- Who are the current members of this family?
- What kinds of people would they describe themselves as?
- How do family members describe themselves racially?
- What good and bad things have happened to them over time?
- What were or are the group's experiences with oppression?
- What lessons have they learned from their experiences?
- What are the ways in which pride and shame are shown in this family?
- Identify the family beliefs in the case. What are your beliefs about how the family functions?
- Design a family ritual or tradition this family can use to reinforce connections.

c. During the interview, the interviewer should be completing the pictorial representation of the cultural genogram and using this to engage the family fully in problem solving. The genogram should illustrate how the family's culture and history play a role in shaping their personal and family values in their current situation.

d. During the interview identify the family strengths and resources. To do this, draw a social network map for the family social support resources. When this is done, evaluate the strength of the support network by completing the Social Network Grid. Consider how suitable the existing informal network is for supporting this family based on the five factors contributing to the structure and functioning of a support network.

e. After the completion of this role play, students as a group should write a brief summary assessment of the family using the following headings:

*Presenting Issues:* Summarize these in one or two sentences.

*Family Membership:* Include the genogram and circle the names of family members living in the home.

*Family Culture:* Indicate in two or three sentences the strength and nature of the cultural bonding among family members.

*Developmental History:* Provide pertinent information concerning family of origin and significant personal, social, vocational, and medical events.

*Strengths/Problems:* Write three sentences to describe family strengths and issues/problems as they relate to family structure—developmental and functional. (Comment on marital system strengths and problems, or parental-child system strengths and problems.)

*Summarize:* Briefly describe the family situation, issues, concerns, and problems.

*Goals and Plans:* Describe an intervention plan or referral; indicate the family's reaction.

f. After the role play and assessment, ask each group to share their observations with the class as a whole. Conclude the exercise by having the large group brainstorm ideas for ways to enhance informal social supports to assist the family.

## Example of a Family Assessment Summary: The Del Sol Family

*Date and Place of Interview:*

*Names of Family Members:*
   *Mother:*
   *Father:*
   *Children:*

*Names of Family Members Present:*

*Interviewer:*

*Presenting Issues:*
   (Brief introduction—e.g., The parents and child attended for an assessment at the Neighborhood Outreach Office as the social worker thought they needed a family assessment. Rosa, the mother, had difficulty managing Christopher, the nine-year-old son from a previous marriage. Christopher would not sit in his chair and insisted on interrupting his parents and the interviewer; he frequently left the room even when Rosa requested that he remain. He kicked the chairs and made irritating noises throughout the session.)

*Family Membership:*
   The family is composed of husband Miguel, 37, a tradesman; wife Rosa, 35, who works part-time in a gardening shop; and children Teresa, 3, Tina, 18 months, and Christopher, the son from a previous relationship. (Draw the genogram here showing membership.)

*Family Attachment:*
   (Draw the genogram here showing strength of attachments between family members.)

*Relevant History:*
   *Children:* All normal development and birth history.

   *Parents:* Both are from families where corporal punishment was used; high levels of family conflict and low levels of nurturing and warmth were demonstrated in family of origin.

   *Family:* Stable but conflictual relationship between the husband and wife; both families of origin provide conflicting advice about child rearing and the marriage.

*Strengths/Problems:*
   *Whole family system:*
      Strengths: Extended family has a high level of involvement in the family. Grandparents may be a source of support.

Problems: Ongoing conflictual relationships with families of origin. Miguel feels particularly angry toward his father and wants to discuss his feelings about his own drinking and its impact on him. Rosa felt abandoned by her father and has questions about why he left her mother. The couple has not found helpful ways to deal with their anger toward their parents.

Isolation: The couple feels they do not have a friendship network and sometimes feel trapped and isolated in the family.

*Marital System:*

Strengths: Both Miguel and Rosa are concerned about their parenting and want to have a good relationship with their children. The couple feels they want to stay together and make the marriage work.

Problems: Both parents have difficulty expressing their feelings to each other and the children. They are unable to express their emotions toward their families.

*Parent-Child System:*

Strengths: Children appear connected to parents; they seem to want more contact and time with father.

Problems: Christopher has behavioral difficulties in home and school. He has few playmates and appears isolated. Rosa feels overwhelmed about child responsibilities and dislikes Miguel's use of corporal punishment and critical attitude toward the children. Miguel is more argumentative when he is drinking.

*Sibling Subsystem:*

Strengths: Christopher likes his sisters and generally gets along with them.

Problems: At times Christopher shows rivalry or jealousy when he takes belongings from his sisters and is aggressive toward them. This is particularly evident when the girls receive attention from Rosa.

*Individual System:*

Strengths: Christopher is a bright child and has a desire to be cooperative. He wants to be involved in sports and other group activities. His early years in school were positive experiences and he can be a cheerful child.

Problems: Christopher is presently experiencing difficulties managing his behavior in acceptable ways both at school and at home.

*Summary:*

Miguel and Rosa are experiencing marital conflict and parent management difficulties, especially with Christopher. Christopher's problem has existed for one year since he was promoted to second grade. He is showing signs of aggression and inability to control his behavior, which is particularly evident when teachers or parents ask him to behave. His parents have resorted to using coercive parenting techniques to get him to behave and often use corporal punishment. The family environment is described as high in criticism and low in warmth and nurturing. The parents have difficulty expressing their feelings of love and caring. One possibility is that Rosa and Miguel's poor parenting models may explain the couple's limited ability to demonstrate positive parenting practices and they have few alternative strategies for teaching positive behaviors to Christopher. Mr. Del Sol has a problem with alcohol, which contributes to the conflict between the couple. The family appears to have positive attachments and a sense of motivation to work on the problems.

*Goals and Plans for Interventions:*

The parents and Christopher have agreed to meet for five sessions to learn how to manage Christopher's behavior.

Parents will have joint meetings with the practitioner to discuss marital communication problems and ways to reduce the stress and tensions in the family environment through examining roles, family structures, and emotional supports. Practitioner will use evaluation measures to determine Miguel's drinking severity.

*Interviewer:*

Muriel Carston, M.S.W.

# Case Study: The Del Sol Family

## Referral Route

Rosa Del Sol was self-referred to the Parkview Family Services agency. At the time of intake, Rosa's presenting concerns were marital conflict and parenting concerns, especially how to manage her nine-year-old son, Christopher.

## Family Composition

The Del Sol family consists of Rosa, age 35, and Miguel, age 37, as well as three children. Rosa and Miguel have been married for four years. Their two daughters are Teresa, age three, and Tina, age 18 months. Christopher, age nine, is Rosa's son from a previous common-law relationship. Christopher's biological father, Jim, age 36, has not been involved in Christopher's life since the child was two years old and Rosa does not know Jim's whereabouts. Rosa states Jim was a heavy drinker and became physically abusive during the pregnancy; they separated shortly after Christopher's birth.

Rosa is the only child of Maria and Don Valdez, age 55 and 60, respectively. Don was verbally and physically abusive toward Maria, and they separated when Rosa was 12 years old. Rosa has had no contact with her biological father since that time. Maria continued to parent Rosa on her own and has not remarried.

Miguel is the oldest son of Sophia and Thomas Del Sol, ages 62 and 66, respectively. Miguel's younger brother, Juan, age 34, is not married and, according to Miguel, has a "drinking problem." Miguel's father "abandoned" the family when Miguel was seven years old. Miguel remembers the loud arguing and fighting between his parents. His mother was remarried, when Miguel was 10 years old, to Ken Wheeler.

## The Del Sol Family Genogram
Each student will complete the genogram.

## The Family System

Rosa was in tears for most of the initial session, claiming she "just can't take it anymore." Miguel is constantly putting her down, insulting her in front of other people (even in the grocery store), and yelling at the children. Rosa feels that no matter what she does she cannot seem to do anything right (according to Miguel). Rosa is beginning to realize that she is being verbally abused as her father abused her mother. She is also very uncomfortable with her reactions because she has been yelling back at Miguel and feels like the "war is on." Rosa feels the situation is "out of control." Sometimes her own anger and Miguel's intensity of anger have frightened her. Physical abuse has not occurred up to this point according to Rosa. She states that Miguel knows if he ever touches her that would be the end of the relationship. She is determined not to raise her children in an "abusive home" like the home of her own childhood. Rosa says she cries frequently and has had little energy to deal with the conflicts Christopher has been having at school as well as the daily "battles" with Miguel.

Miguel feels the problems between him and Rosa can be "solved on their own." Miguel admits that he yells a lot at Rosa and calls her names. However, he points out that he always tells Rosa he is sorry. Miguel is of average height and slim build; he appeared very agitated and tense. He admits to experiencing a number of physical symptoms of stress including a pounding heart, frequent headaches, and constant feelings of edginess and restlessness. Miguel describes himself as a loner with no close friends. Miguel agrees with Rosa that he is moody but "a guy can't be in a good mood all of the time." Miguel's posture and manner appeared defensive and he indicated he was here only because Rosa had threatened to leave him if they didn't get help. His family is important to him and he realizes now that despite not wanting to repeat the actions of his stepfather, he can see that he is doing the same to his children.

Christopher attends Parkview School and is in grade two. He is in a regular class after having repeated grade one. Christopher was diagnosed with Attention Deficit Disorder (ADD) six months ago. He is currently on a trial of Ritalin. In the past month, the school has complained to Rosa that Christopher has become increasingly aggressive with his peers. Christopher's teacher reported that he has made no friends in his class and has become socially isolated, either withdrawing or acting out angrily. The teacher noted that Christopher had poor social skills but was quite good in sport activities such as soccer and hockey. Christopher's favorite winter sport is hockey and in the summer he loves to swim, play soccer, and ride his bike.

Three-year-old Teresa is a talkative girl who is generally good-natured. Tina, 18 months, tends to be quiet and allows Teresa to do all the talking for her. Both girls have been achieving their respective developmental milestones. Rosa has no concerns in this area. However, she has noticed in the past three weeks that both girls have not been sleeping through the night. They have been whining and crying a lot more than usual. Teresa has been complaining of a stomachache frequently. Rosa became upset when she told about Miguel coming home from work and marching into the bedroom in silence, and Teresa asking, "Is Daddy mad again?"

## Family Background Information

Rosa completed grade 12 and then worked in a bank as a teller until the birth of Teresa. Her mother helped her raise Christopher when he was an infant and openly stated her disapproval of Rosa's relationship with Jim, Christopher's father. Maria lives nearby and, despite what Rosa describes as a "conflictual" relationship, is a source of support for Rosa. Maria often baby-sits the girls, although Maria now refuses to look after Christopher because "he is too difficult—just like his father." Rosa describes the relationship between her mother and Miguel as "unfriendly"; "they tolerate one another" as each tends to put the other down. Rosa feels stuck in the middle of a "no win" situation.

Miguel never got along with his stepfather, Ken. Ken frequently became drunk on the weekends with Sophia, leaving the boys to fend for themselves. Ken was not physically abusive, but when he was drinking "you stayed out of his way so he wouldn't yell at you." Miguel says his mother, Sophia, is an alcoholic and he has chosen not to have contact with her or with his stepfather. Miguel quit school and left home at age 15. He worked at odd jobs to support himself. Miguel admits to "being in the wrong crowd" and heavily involved with drugs and alcohol as a teenager. Miguel feels proud that he is no longer involved "in that scene" having quit on his own "without anyone's help."

## Family Strengths and Challenges

### Stress or Demand Factors

*Family System*  All family members appear to be suffering from symptoms of stress both physically and/or emotionally and have experienced a number of changes recently. The purchase of their own home with the resulting high mortgage payments has left little money to cover remaining bills and groceries. The lack of money and high debt load has become a daily stressor. Rosa and Miguel agree that, on a regular basis, most of their arguments are precipitated by financial issues.

Christopher's recent diagnosis of ADD is confusing to Miguel and Rosa. They have little information on this disorder or how best to deal with Christopher in managing his behaviors appropriately.

*Marital/Parental Subsystem*  Miguel has a grade-school education and is employed full time at a small auto repair shop. He also works a second job in an auto parts store in the evenings and weekends to make ends meet. Miguel complains about his co-workers, stating he has nothing in common with them and doesn't want to waste his time with them. Miguel feels his boss is always pressuring him to do more and they often have loud disagreements. Miguel aspires to be a manager of his own shop and not have people telling him what to do.

Miguel and Rosa purchased their home four months ago. It is located about 45 minutes by car from their old neighborhood where Rosa was well connected to the church and a number of friends. The couple enjoy owning their own home; however, the mortgage payments are very high. This leaves little money for other expenses and has been a source of conflict on a daily basis.

Rosa and Miguel had decided that Rosa would stay home to care for the girls while they were young. Lately, however, Rosa has been suggesting that she work part-time outside to help out financially and to be out of the house. Miguel then could cut down on his hours of work and spend time with the family. Miguel reacted angrily to this suggestion and stated that he was "sick and tired of everyone hassling him about working and can't a guy just make a living." Miguel works hard at his two jobs and is very committed to doing the best for his family. However, all his energies have been devoted to making a living, with little time for any outside interests. Rosa feels money is less of an issue than Miguel and would rather have him spend time with her and the children as a family. Miguel admits he is getting physically tired and irritable and finds he is less able to handle life's minor annoyances. He would like to be able to spend time with the children and get back into playing recreational hockey.

*Parent-Child Subsystem*    Student is to complete this.

*Sibling Subsystem*    Student is to complete this.

*Resource Factors*    Rosa described herself as an outgoing, social person with a sense of humor but lately she has been feeling alone and "down." The family has one car that Miguel uses to travel to work, and Rosa feels isolated and "stuck in the house."

The family have few outside supports. Rosa, due to the move and transportation limitations, is isolated from her previous support network, which included neighborhood friends and the church community. Miguel has very few friends and relies on Rosa to be his constant cheerleader to make him feel good. Rosa has said it feels at times that she has four children, not three. The girls don't have friends in the new neighborhood because the children living nearby are much older. The girls are becoming quite bored and cranky, with Rosa adding to the tension in the home. Christopher has made a couple of new friends; however, his poor social skills and short attention span has made this a challenge for him.

*Competence and Coping Factors*    Rosa grew up in an abusive home and is determined to not raise her children in that environment. She is very motivated to make changes in her life and has attempted over the last year to involve Miguel in activities to strengthen their family; he has refused to attend any couple enrichment weekends or courses that were available at no cost through the church. Rosa attended the sessions on her own, including a weekend retreat for families.

Rosa has a wonderful sense of humor that has helped her cope with a number of adverse conditions. Rosa feels she has no support from Miguel in raising the children due to his drive to make money and his discomfort at being with the children. Rosa is a good mother to her children and is determined to continue to learn about positive parenting approaches.

Miguel is a hard worker and he feels he must do the very best with any job he takes on. High expectations create added pressure and stress. Miguel has been reluctant to tackle areas in which he feels incompetent. These include parenting, so he tends to avoid it when he can, often choosing work over time with the family.

Miguel grew up in an abusive alcoholic family and exhibits some of the symptoms common to this environment, such as poor self-image, a need for constant approval, and repressed anger. He believes strongly that the husband's role is to provide for his family. Miguel has difficulty recognizing that his family has other needs from a husband and father than just money. This pattern was established in his family of origin. His strong desire to raise his children differently and to keep his family together will help him in achieving his goals.

## Planning for Services

Miguel and Rosa decided upon the following goals:

1. To develop appropriate strategies for managing anger and developing effective, respectful communication
2. To deal more effectively with managing stress
3. To expand the current support network of their family
4. To increase their understanding of Attention Deficit Disorder and parenting techniques

## Assessment Tools

Assessment evaluation tools, such as the Hudson Scales–Index of Family Relations, Index of Clinical Stress, Partner Abuse Scale (Non-physical), and Generalized Contentment Scale, will be used to monitor progress and severity of the identified issues for the couple. Christopher will be asked to complete the Index of Family Relations. Questions directed to Rosa regarding Teresa and Tina with respect to sleep patterns, eating patterns, physical complaints, and mood will be used to monitor their levels of stress. As well, ongoing verbal feedback will be requested from all members of the family.

## Interventions

Miguel has been suffering physical symptoms of stress so was referred to his family doctor for a complete physical examination to rule out any other causes. Miguel will contact his doctor within the week to book the appointment.

Rosa will explore part-time employment to relieve financial stress, gain a sense of independence, increase her self-esteem, and expand her support network within the workplace to decrease her sense of isolation.

Rosa will research activities available in the neighborhood such as mom and tot mornings to assist in expanding her network as well as that of the girls, decrease isolation, and give her a break from the children. She will also contact her mother to see if Maria would look after the girls one or two mornings a week while Christopher is in school so Rosa could spend some time pursuing activities that are important to her. Miguel is to pick an activity he would like to do for himself (such as recreational hockey) and schedule a time weekly to participate.

Rosa and Miguel, with Christopher's input, will explore activities to increase his physical activity, expand his experiences interacting with peers, and allow opportunities for Miguel to spend time with Christopher. Activities suggested for

Christopher that Miguel might assist with were joining a hockey team, beginning a swimming program, and/or becoming a Boy Scout.

Rosa and Miguel were informed that financial support is available through different programs and memorial funds to help them to involve their children in community activities. Teresa and Tina could participate in tot programs at the community center, church, local swimming pool, and other facilities.

Rosa and Miguel will attend the church in their new neighborhood to begin building the family's network within the church community. In their previous neighborhood, the church hel sessions on a regular basis, which Miguel refused to attend, on enriching family life and learning child development and parenting approaches. However, Miguel has agreed to attend these sessions due to his concern over keeping the family together, and there is no charge. Miguel and Rosa will explore the programs at the new church.

Rosa and Miguel were provided with resources for information and support related to Attention Deficit Disorder and parenting a child with ADD. Parent support groups can provide ongoing support and offer parents updated information in areas such as treatment, medications, and new resource materials.

Rosa and Miguel will attend an anger management group program that includes stress management and communication skills; it also provides child care at no charge. If baby sitting is a problem, Rosa will check with her neighbor(s) to see if she could set up a small baby sitting co-op.

Following the completion of the initial treatment, other programs are available that could be beneficial for Rosa and Miguel as well as support meetings to help them maintain the gains made.

## Evaluation

Evaluation tools such as the Hudson Scales–Index of Family Relations, Index of Clinical Stress, Partner Abuse Scale (Non-physical), and Generalized Contentment Scale will be used to monitor progress and severity of the identified issues for the couple. Christopher will be asked to complete the Index of Family Relations. Questions directed to Rosa regarding Teresa and Tina with respect to sleep patterns, eating patterns, physical complaints, and mood will be used to monitor their levels of stress in the family. As well, ongoing verbal feedback will be requested from all members of the family.

## Contract

Miguel and Rosa contracted to

- Attend an anger management group for 20 sessions.
- Involve each member of the family in an activity.
- Plan a family outing (e.g., picnic, day at the lake).
- Contact resources regarding A.D.D. and parenting.

The student will complete the contract for services.

▼▼▼

# CHAPTER TEN

# The McCoy Family: Coping With a Mother's Death

With the following case study, you can learn about assessing a family as well as practice and discuss family assessment. Study questions and exercises may be done independently as a form of self-study or in peer group learning situations. Some exercises are more relevant than others to the work of particular individuals and groups. Remember that different and creative responses are acceptable as you plan interventions. The basis of this case is from my practice/research but it is essentially a composite of child and family situations.

## Study Activities

Not all items will apply to the case, but all included here are to stimulate your thinking about family assessment and intervention.

1. What are the family issues?
2. What are the family and individual needs for

   - Concrete, instrumental support?
   - Information, knowledge and skills?
   - Emotional supports?
   - Affiliational supports?

3. Analyze the family system:

   a. Examine the family member boundaries—a critical task in determining family interaction patterns, roles and power, and parenting issues. Describe the boundaries, interaction patterns, roles and power, and parenting issues in the case.

   b. Describe the situation in the family regarding

- Emotional connections
- Resources within the family

   c. Describe what a family-centered approach will look like in this family

   d. Answer the following questions about the family unit in this case:

- What systems are apparent at the individual and family level?
- What functions are performed by which family systems and how well do the systems function?
- Do any boundaries need to be changed? What needs to be done? Describe how you will do this.
- What are the family system strengths and problems?
- Family behaviors are best understood from a circular causality rather than a linear causality. Using an example from this case, where might you use a circular perspective to make a cognitive change, affective change, or behavioral change?
- What are examples of risk factors in this case?
- What are examples of strengths in this case?
- What stage of development is the family in?
- What are the tasks associated with this stage of development?
- What are the stressors associated with the tasks?
- How have the stressors impacted family development?
- What events have impacted the family structure and family membership at this stage?

4. *Family Assessment:* The goal of this activity is to document and develop knowledge of the culture of the McCoy family. Several tasks are required and approximately two hours will be needed to complete this group activity, which starts with a role play of a family interview. The class can be divided into small groups, each engaging in a family interview role play; another option is for one small group to role-play, with other classmates observing and recording, followed by large group discussion. Be sure to have a flip chart available to document or illustrate the cultural genogram or social network map, and have a copy of the social network grid for this interview.

   a. Students should assume the roles of the McCoy family members (Ed, father; and Tamara, Kayla, and Kyle, the children) and an interviewer.

   b. This is the first interview with the McCoy family and the focus of the family meeting is on obtaining information related to the family's culture and history. Questions to consider for the cultural assessment follow:

- Where did the family come from?
- When did they come to this country?
- What were the circumstances that brought them to this country?
- What is important to this family?
- Who are the current members of this family?
- What kinds of people would they describe themselves as?
- How do family members describe themselves racially?
- What good and bad things have happened to them over time?
- What were or are the group's experiences with oppression?
- What lessons have they learned from their experiences?
- What are the ways in which pride and shame are shown in this family?
- Identify the family beliefs in the case. What are your beliefs about how the family functions?
- Design a family ritual or tradition this family can use to reinforce connections.

c. During the interview, the interviewer should be completing the pictorial representation of the cultural genogram and using this to engage the family fully in problem solving. The genogram should illustrate how the family's culture and history play a role in shaping their personal and family values in their current situation.

d. During the interview identify the family strengths and resources. To do this, draw a social network map for the family social support resources. When this is done, evaluate the strength of the support network by completing the Social Network Grid. Consider how suitable the existing informal network is for supporting this family based on the five factors contributing to the structure and functioning of a support network.

e. After the completion of this role play, students as a group should write a brief summary assessment of the family using the following headings:

*Presenting Issues:* Summarize these in one or two sentences.

*Family Membership:* Include the genogram and circle the names of family members living in the home.

*Family Culture:* Indicate in two or three sentences the strength and nature of the cultural bonding among family members.

*Developmental History:* Provide pertinent information concerning family of origin and significant personal, social, vocational, and medical events.

*Strengths/Problems:* Write three sentences to describe family strengths and issues/problems as they relate to family structure-developmental and functional. (Comment on marital strengths and problems.)

*Summarize:* Briefly describe the family situation, issues, concerns, and problems.

*Goals and Plans:* Describe an intervention plan-or referral; indicate the family's reaction.

f. After the role play and assessment, ask each group to share their observations with the class as a whole. Conclude the exercise by having the large group brainstorm ideas for ways to enhance informal social supports to assist the family.

# Case Study: The McCoy Family

## Referral Route

Mr. Ed McCoy was referred to the Children's Hospital for counseling by the family doctor following the death of his wife. The problem Mr. McCoy identified, at the time of intake, was his need for assistance in adjusting to parenting without his partner.

## Family Composition

The McCoy family consists of Mr. McCoy, age 36, and his three children: Tamara, age 10; Kayla, age 8; and Kyle, age 4. Mrs. Tina McCoy died approximately three months ago from a connective tissue disorder. Mrs. McCoy was the youngest of two children, born to Grace and John Redding. John died at the age of 50, from heart disease, 20 years ago. Grace, age 68, retired two years ago from teaching. She was recently diagnosed with cancer. Mrs. Redding lives in the same city and has always been involved with her grandchildren. She frequently baby sits the three children. It is unknown how her involvement with the children will be affected because of the change in her health status.

Mrs. McCoy had one older sister, with whom she shared a very close relationship. Rhonda, age 38, is married and living in the same city as the McCoys. Rhonda has a daughter, age 12, and a son, age 11. Rhonda works full time in a professional position that frequently requires long hours. Rhonda has also been quite involved in the children's lives and has offered to raise the McCoy children for Mr. McCoy. Mr. McCoy describes his relationship with his sister-in-law as conflictual.

Mr. Ed McCoy, age 36, is the eldest of two children born to Edwin and Katherine McCoy. Edwin died from heart disease at the age of 58. He was a university professor. Katherine, age 60, is described as healthy and active. As she lives in another state, she does not visit often, and she has a distant relationship with her son and grandchildren.

Mr. McCoy's younger sister, Patricia, age 30, is recently married and lives close to her mother. She also has a somewhat distant relationship with her brother and his family.

## The McCoy Family Genogram

Each student will complete the genogram.

## The Family System

The entire McCoy family was identified as the client system. This includes Ed, Tamara, Kayla, and Kyle.

Mr. McCoy is a tall, slim, attractive man. He appears somewhat unkempt and frequently seems distracted. He has a college diploma and has been steadily employed for the last 16 years. Currently he is employed full time by a large oil company as a computer technician. He has some degree of flexibility in his work, but has established the pattern of working long hours and occasional weekends.

Tamara, age 10, is presently in grade five at Woodview Elementary School. She has long, brown hair, is a straight "A" student, and appears to be a quiet and compliant little girl. She appears to have shouldered a great deal of additional responsibility during her mother's illness and since her death. During the initial interviews with the McCoy family, Mr. McCoy applauded Tamara for being a good little mother when she took charge of her younger brother after he became restless in the session.

Kayla, age 8, is in grade three at Woodview Elementary School. She has short dark hair and an engaging grin. She is tall and quite thin and could be described as loose-limbed. She apparently looks most like her mother, and Mr. McCoy fears she may have some of the characteristics that would indicate a possible connective tissue disorder. The genetics department at Children's Hospital will be investigating this possibility. Mr. McCoy indicates that Kayla is the child that he finds most challenging. She is quite active, questions decisions openly, and frequently does not comply with her father's wishes. Mr. McCoy feels that his wife was better able to manage Kayla and that she was the child closest to her mother. Kayla, who has always been an average student, has also experienced some difficulties at school since the death of her mother. She has not been completing her homework, has had difficulty focusing, and has been at the center of several conflicts with peers. Mr. McCoy is feeling overwhelmed since the death of his wife and has asked the school to manage the behavior, as much as possible.

Kyle, age 4, is enrolled in a community preschool program three mornings per week. He is a charming, engaging boy who appears to be quite content. He looks to his sisters for comfort and support. Kyle's grandmother, Mrs. Redding, has been looking after him during the day since the death of his mother. Mrs. Redding also frequently keeps him overnight when his father works overtime.

## Family Background Information

Mr. McCoy describes his upbringing as very structured. His parents had high expectations for his academic achievements, which he did not fulfill. Mr. McCoy indicates that his parents were not openly affectionate with each other or with the children. Discipline for misbehavior usually meant being confined to the home for short periods of time. Mr. McCoy feels that he parents in a style similar to that of his parents. He is not sure if this style of parenting will be beneficial to his children as they mourn the loss of their mother.

Mr. McCoy's father died suddenly, two years ago, as a result of heart disease. Mr. McCoy did not have an opportunity to see his father before he died. As the relationship had been distant for some time, it had been approximately eight months since his last contact with his father.

## Developmental History of the Family

(The student will complete this.) Include significant events, including the chronological sequence of events leading to the current presenting problem (previous attempts to cope and professional help) as well as families of origin events, and personal, social, vocational, and medical events impacting current functioning.

## Family Strengths and Challenges

### Stress or Demand Factors

*Family System*   Mrs. McCoy died approximately six weeks ago from a genetically inherited connective tissue disorder. This disorder was diagnosed one year ago when Mrs. McCoy began experiencing health difficulties. Because of complications from the disorder, Mrs. McCoy's health deteriorated quickly over the last year, ending in heart failure. She was hospitalized much of the last year and as her condition deteriorated more quickly than at first anticipated, Mr. McCoy feels that neither he nor his wife was able to assist the children adequately in coping with her illness.

Mr. McCoy feels somewhat distant from his children and has been relying heavily on outside resources to assist him in his parenting responsibilities. With support, it is anticipated that he will be able to provide adequately for his children both emotionally and functionally. There appears to be some role confusion for both the children and Mr. McCoy. Tamara is taking on some of the household and nurturing tasks while Mr. McCoy appears to be relinquishing his parent role to others outside the home. Even the school is attempting to be helpful by not involving Mr. McCoy in some potentially serious difficulties that Kayla is experiencing. The risk for Mr. McCoy is that if he doesn't take charge of his family and feel some degree of confidence in his ability to provide for them, he will, by default, lose any position of authority in the family.

Another factor impacting the family is how both Mrs. Redding and her daughter Rhonda are dealing with the loss of their daughter and sister. In their attempts to cope, they are undermining the role of Mr. McCoy. However, both grandmother and aunt could potentially be a tremendous support for the McCoy family.

*Marital/Parental Subsystem*   Prior to Tina's illness and her subsequent death, Mr. McCoy indicated that there had been a great deal of conflict in the relationship. Mrs. McCoy had expressed a desire to return to work and had requested that Mr. McCoy share some of the child care responsibilities to enable her to do this. Mr. McCoy had argued that his role was that of the "breadwinner" and that all other responsibilities had fallen to his wife. Mr. McCoy expresses sadness and a sense of loss at the death of his partner.

Mr. McCoy appears to have come from a disengaged family system, where boundaries and family ties were not always clear. His own father was not actively involved in the parenting role and there were likely issues outstanding between father and son at the time of the older Mr. McCoy's death. Mr. Ed McCoy's attitude toward parenting is much the same as his father's but he is now being forced to take a more active role.

*Parent-Child Subsystem*    It is common to see blurring of generational boundaries in single-parent systems, and it is already apparent in the McCoy family as Tamara takes on adult responsibilities in the household and parental responsibilities regarding her youngest sibling. The family would also expect to become isolated while grieving their loss. In the McCoy family, the opposite seems to be occurring. The family seems to be becoming more disengaged and losing some of its identity as a distinct unit.

*Sibling Subsystem*    The student is to complete this.

*Resource Factors*    The McCoys are a loving family who have suffered the loss of their wife/mother. A number of supports exist within the system. Mrs. Redding, the maternal grandmother, and Rhonda, Mrs. McCoy's sister, are both involved and supportive of the children. Mr. McCoy also indicates that several neighbors and parents of his children's friends have been supportive and offered to help—particularly with the two girls. Staff at the school the girls attend have also extended an offer to assist in whatever way possible. They have already demonstrated their willingness to help by not contacting Mr. McCoy with continuing concerns regarding Kayla and attempting to deal with the issues without Mr. McCoy's input.

Mr. McCoy enjoys stable employment, with some degree of flexibility. He is bright, caring, and open to input on how best to assist his children in coping with the loss of their mother. Mr. McCoy has been managing household tasks by hiring help. He indicates that this is not a good long-term solution because of the cost, but he feels that short term it is worth the additional financial burden.

While having support from Mrs. McCoy's family has been a very real advantage for Mr. McCoy, he has found that Mrs. Redding and Rhonda have been making more of the decisions than he has regarding the children and he feels less and less important in his own children's life as time goes by. Rhonda's offer to parent the children appears to have been threatening rather than comforting to Mr. McCoy, as it raised doubts in him about his competence as a parent.

*Competence and Coping Factors*    The family system demonstrates a number of strengths including their caring and affection for each other, Mr. McCoy's ability to reach out to the community for assistance, his stable employment, and the support of the extended family and the community in general.

## Recommendations for Family Work

The McCoy family has been seen for two sessions and has contracted for an additional five sessions. Grieving and loss for both the children and Mr. McCoy is an issue of central importance. The primary reason for changes in family roles and for the number of individuals outside the family who have assumed roles within the family relates to the loss of Mrs. McCoy. Assisting the children to talk openly about their mother; helping them to recall the importance and significance of her presence in their lives; addressing how their needs will be taken care of in the immediate future; and dealing with their sadness and feelings of rejection, loss, and anger is necessary at this time. In order for the children to be able to do these things, they require an available adult who will allow them to grieve and ask questions at their own pace. The children's differing ability to comprehend the death of their mother due to their various developmental levels will also be a factor. For Mr. McCoy to be available, he requires support and an opportunity to work through some of his own issues regarding the death of his wife. Mr. McCoy requires assistance in dealing with both his sadness and his ambivalence regarding the loss of his wife.

Kayla most clearly appears to be demonstrating anxiety about the death of her mother. Her anxiety is more openly displayed through behavior that Mr. McCoy is finding more and more difficult to cope with. Although Kayla has a history of difficult behavior, it was apparently managed quite effectively by Mrs. McCoy. There is an underlying anxiety that Kayla, due to her physical attributes, may have the same illness that her mother died from. Kayla, her siblings, and her father all see Kayla as most like her mother. This belief, which is widely held, may have already influenced Kayla's belief about her own longevity.

## Planning for Services

Mr. McCoy identified the following goals:

1. To assist the family in mourning the death of Mrs. McCoy.
2. To assist Mr. McCoy with the responsibilities of parenting as a single parent.

Mr. McCoy felt that he would know when he no longer required counseling because he would feel more in control and less overwhelmed by the tasks of mourning and parenting. He indicated that managing resources, such as the school and his in-laws, was also a concern for him in his role as a single parent.

Assessment evaluation tools used included the Generalized Contentment Scale and the Index of Family Relations (Hudson Scales). These measures were completed by Mr. McCoy, Tamara, and Kayla. Kyle drew a picture of his family while the others completed these measures. The Adult-Adolescent Parenting Inventory (AAPI) was used to establish a baseline for Mr. McCoy's attitudes regarding parenting.

## Intervention Choices

Family counseling has been chosen as the counseling modality for the McCoys for the following reasons:

1. To reinforce generational boundaries. Mr. McCoy will be given information about parenting roles and responsibilities, and supportive services will be explored:

   - Is there a possibility of grandparenting support, and if so, how much?
   - Are other caregivers available to assume some responsibility to lighten Mr. McCoy's burden?

2. To serve as a model for Mr. McCoy in addressing issues of sadness and loss in the family. Mr. McCoy can be supported in answering the children's questions about their mother's death and provided with a model on how to address difficult questions about the children's grief. Mourning behaviors,

such as school difficulties, can be normalized and strategies for dealing with difficulties can be generated.

3. To support Mr. McCoy's involvement with his children. Seeing the family as a whole helps to redefine the family unit. It will also assist the family in deciding what tasks need to be done and if help from outside the immediate membership would be appropriate.

The focus of the sessions will be on assisting the family to grieve. The initial sessions will explore the death and funeral; the next sessions will focus on the past and memories of Mrs. McCoy; and the final sessions will provide an opportunity for the family to explore the present and the future. The goal of grief counseling is to develop the ability to express both joy at having known the deceased and sadness at the loss. It would be anticipated that the children and their father will grieve the loss of their mother/wife at future developmental stages. The initial grief work provides permission and a model for future grief work.

For this family, the grief work should include discussions of the same qualities the children shared with their mother as well as the ways they were different. This is a technique commonly used to assist the survivors in expressing qualities they admired about the deceased. It is a technique also used to differentiate between getting sick and dying from cancer and getting sick with a cold. Looking at differences can delineate how Kayla is different and how even if she has the same diagnosis as her mother, she may not follow the same course her mother did.

In addition to family counseling, Mr. McCoy will be referred to the Widows/Widowers Association to join an open-ended support group to help him deal with the loss of his partner. Again, this reinforces the need for Mr. McCoy to have ongoing support for himself, apart from the children. The group will also normalize the range of emotion Mr. McCoy feels at the death of his wife and provide some support for his ongoing parenting struggles.

Mr. McCoy expressed a desire to receive support in his single parenting role. It is recommended that Mr. McCoy be seen individually every second week or that he contract for further counseling once family counseling is completed. Individual counseling will provide Mr. McCoy with the opportunity to explore his role as a single parent, how he can support Kayla at home and at school, and how he can include extended family and friends in his support network. Mr. McCoy will be made aware of parenting resources in his area for future reference. In the months following a death it is important to minimize the number of other changes that might occur for the family. As Mr. McCoy's in-laws have been very involved in the children's lives, assisting Mr. McCoy in his relationship with them could be a focus of the counseling. Working on how to address the concerns of his sister-in-law, reframing her actions as an indication of caring and setting boundaries in the relationship, will provide the basis for an ongoing source of support from the extended family.

## Evaluation

Services will be evaluated after the five sessions that follow the assessment period. The evaluation will be based on written and verbal feedback from Mr. McCoy on symptoms associated with grieving, such as sleeping and eating patterns in the family, ability to focus on work or school tasks, openness to talking about Mrs. McCoy by family members, ability to formulate goals and plans for the family, and the degree to which Mr. McCoy continues to feel overwhelmed.

The measures identified above, including the Generalized Contentment Scale and the Index of Family Relations (Hudson Scales), will be repeated by Mr. McCoy, Tamara, and Kayla at the completion of the five family sessions. Kyle will again be asked to draw a picture of his family while the others are completing the measures. The Adult-Adolescent Parenting Inventory (AAPI) will also be used to chart Mr. McCoy's changing attitudes and level of confidence regarding parenting.

## Notes on Contracting

Contracting for counseling services occurred at two different points with the McCoy family and will occur again on completion of the five family counseling sessions. Contracting began at the telephone intake when Mr. McCoy requested services. He was asked some preliminary questions by the screener and then it was agreed that a therapist would contact him directly to arrange an appointment. When contacted, Mr. McCoy agreed to an initial session to discuss his need for services. Initial sessions usually begin with therapists describing their professional background, their working style, and any relevant agency policies and procedures. This would include issues of confidentiality, payment for counseling, and the right of the client to request a different therapist.

Mr. McCoy was then given an opportunity to discuss what he was hoping to receive from counseling. He talked about feeling overwhelmed by the enormity of the tasks facing him and about a sense of helplessness in knowing what to do first and how to do it. He indicated he was looking for support and concrete suggestions.

Mr. McCoy agreed to two assessment sessions at which time the therapist would make recommendations for future services. This would also give Mr. McCoy an opportunity to indicate whether the sessions to date had been helpful and to articulate what he believes would be helpful for future sessions.

Following the initial two sessions Mr. McCoy indicated that he would like additional support and that the recommendation for five family sessions would be helpful. He particularly liked how his position as head of the family was reinforced and he appreciated the therapist's supporting him in that role, at the same time giving specific cues as to appropriate responses to the children. This allowed Mr. McCoy to feel competent and increased his confidence. Mr. McCoy also indicated that he would like to think about the variety of options presented regarding individual support for himself. The support group for widows and widowers was of particular interest, but still sounded too threatening at this point. Mr. McCoy indicated that he would be open to discussing this option at a later time.

# CHAPTER ELEVEN

# The Yellowbird Family: A Troubled Child

The case study of the Yellowbird family provides opportunities for you to learn about assessing a family as well as to practice and discuss family assessment. Study questions and exercises may be done independently as a form of self-study or in peer group learning situations. Some exercises are more relevant than others to the work of particular individuals and groups. Remember that different and creative responses are acceptable as you plan interventions. The basis of this case is from my practice/research, but it is essentially a composite of child and family situations.

## Study Activities

Not all items will apply to the case, but all included here are to stimulate your thinking about family assessment and intervention.

1. What are the family issues?
2. What are the family and individual needs for

   - Concrete, instrumental support?
   - Information, knowledge, and skills?
   - Emotional supports?
   - Affiliational supports?

3. Analyze the family system:

   a. Examine the family member boundaries—a critical task in determining family interaction patterns, roles and power, and parenting issues. Describe the boundaries, interaction patterns, roles and power, and parenting issues in the case.

   b. Describe the situation in the family regarding

      ● Emotional connections.
      ● Resources within the family.

   c. Describe what a family-centered approach will look like in this family.

   d. Answer the following questions about the family unit in this case:

      ● What systems are apparent at the individual and family level?
      ● What functions are performed by which family systems and how well do the systems function?
      ● Do any boundaries need to be changed? What needs to be done? Describe how you will do this.
      ● What are the family system strengths and problems?
      ● Family behaviors are best understood from a circular causality rather than a linear causality. Using an example from this case, where might you use a circular perspective to make a cognitive change, affective change, or behavioral change?
      ● What are examples of risk factors in this case?
      ● What are examples of strengths in this case?
      ● What stage of development is the family in?
      ● What are the tasks associated with this stage of development?
      ● What are the stressors associated with the tasks?
      ● How have the stressors impacted family development?
      ● What events have impacted the family structure and family membership at this stage?

4. *Family Assessment:* The goal of this activity is to document and develop knowledge of the culture of the Yellowbird family. Several tasks are required, and approximately two hours will be needed to complete this group activity, which starts with a role play of a family interview. The class can be divided into small groups, each engaging in a family interview role play; another option is for one small group to role-play, with other classmates observing and recording, followed by large group discussion. Be sure to have a flip chart available to document or illustrate the cultural genogram or social network map, and have a copy of the social network grid for this review.

   a. Students should assume the roles of the Yellowbird family members (Stone, father; Carol, mother; and Jason, age 13) and an interviewer.

   b. This is the first interview with the Yellowbird family and the focus if the family meeting is on obtaining information related to the family's culture and history. Questions to consider for the cultural assessment follow:

- Where did the family come from?
- When did they come to this country?
- What were the circumstances that brought them to this country?
- What is important to this family?
- Who are the current members of this family?
- What kind of people would they describe themselves as?
- How do family members describe themselves racially?
- What good and bad things have happened to them over time?
- What were or are the group's experiences with oppression?
- What lessons have they learned from their experiences?
- What are the ways in which pride and shame issues are shown in this family?
- Identify the family beliefs in the case? What are your beliefs about how the family functions?

c. During the interview, the interviewer should be completing the pictorial representation of the cultural genogram and using this to engage the family fully in problem solving. The genogram should illustrate how the family's culture and history play a role in shaping their personal and family values in their current situation.

d. During the interview, identify the family strengths and resources. To do this, draw a social network map for the family social support resources. When this is done, evaluate the strength of the support network by completing the Social Network Grid. Consider how suitable the existing informal support network is for supporting this family based on the five factors contributing to the structure and functioning of a support network.

e. After the completion of this role play, students as a group should write a brief summary assessment of the family using the following headings:

*Presenting Issues:* Summarize these in tone or two sentences.

*Family Membership:* Include the genogram and circle the names of family members living in the home.

*Family Culture:* Indicate in two or three sentences the strength and nature of the cultural bonding among family members.

*Developmental History:* Provide pertinent information concerning family origin and significant personal, social, vocational, and medical events.

*Strength/Problems:* Write three sentences to describe family strengths and issues/problems as they relate to family structure—developmental and functional (Comment on marital system strengths and problems, or parental-child system strengths and problems.)

*Summarize:* Briefly describe the family situation, issues, concerns, and problems.

> *Goals and Plans:* Describe an intervention plan—or referral; indicate the family's reaction.

f.  After the role play and assessment, ask each group to share their observations with the class as a hole. Conclude the exercise by having the large group brainstorm ideas for ways to enhance informal social supports to assist the family.

# Case Study: The Yellowbird Family

## Referral Source

Issues of abuse and neglect had prompted the referral of Jason Yellowbird, age eight, and his family for child protective services. The Child Welfare Placement, Assessment and Review Committee (PARC) recommended that Jason be placed into treatment foster care following a six-month placement at the W. H. Hatton Center for emotionally disturbed children. By age nine, Jason was served by the Valleyview Treatment Foster Family Care program. Following a short-term placement in treatment foster care, Jason was reunited with his mother and stepfather even though the parents were initially hostile to this idea. Eventually, Jason entered the criminal justice system and a second period of treatment foster care was recommended. Now 13 years old, Jason has begun to live with Sue and Brian Lasting, treatment foster care parents with the Valleyview program. Jason remains in contact with his mother Carol and stepfather Jeff. The long-term goal of the second placement in treatment foster family care was to prepare Jason to return to his parents.

## Family Composition

Jason Yellowbird, age 13, is the son of Carol and Stone Yellowbird. Carol, age 31 at the time of Jason's second treatment foster care placement, divorced Stone when Jason was four years old. Carol and Stone had married when she was 17 years old and pregnant with Jason. Jason has had only intermittent contact with his biological father.

No other information is known about the family.

## The Yellowbird Family Genogram

The student will complete this.

## Family Background Information

Carol didn't much like the idea of Jason being in the W. H. Hatton Center as she had spent her teenage years in an institution herself. However, after a childhood with an alcoholic father and a rejecting mother, and after an early and disastrous first marriage to Jason's father, having Jason in out-of-home care was the only peace she had ever had.

With Jason in out-of-home care, Jeff, too, was enjoying his first taste of a stable lifestyle. His own mother had died when he was a child, and he had lived with his grandparents until his father remarried. He had then returned to his father but his stepmother had not wanted Jeff. She had made it very clear that she didn't want Jeff, and that was why Jeff, as a stepfather, had done his best for Jason.

## Placement Background Information

Jason Yellowbird, at the age of eight, was mean and tough. He boasted, he argued, he broke things—his own and other people's. He lied, stole, cheated, and bullied his schoolmates. He hit out at his mother and sometimes at his mother's husband. He knew that people thought he was a bad boy. His mother's husband didn't like him very much. No one liked him very much. Moreover, he wasn't allowed to say that he felt lonely and confused sometimes. Carol didn't like him to say how he felt. Jeff liked him to do as he was told.

Jason's teacher had put him in a short-term observation program at school, which didn't help. Jason continued his life as a tough guy, occasionally becoming a baby. During his times as a baby, he clung to adults and demanded their attention and sometimes soiled his pants. He could read, though, and he could count, and he liked to write. For a kid in grade four, as far as his school work went, Jason was doing all right.

Carol approached a center she knew about that took children like Jason. The children lived together in cottages and were disciplined and cared for. It would be good for Jason, Carol thought, and it might keep her marriage together. Jeff, her second husband, didn't hit her and Jason, as her first husband had. In fact, Jeff had adopted Jason to make her happy, but enough was enough. Jeff was tired of Jason. Carol was tired of Jason. Carol and Jeff were fighting daily over Jason. Jason had to go. Jason was out of control. In summarizing their thoughts about eight-year-old Jason, his mother and stepfather concluded, "This kid is crazy!"

Jason was one of 68 residents at the center for emotionally disturbed children. He was accepted into the residential treatment center under a custody by agreement order. The order said that he would go home in six months, but in six months, his parents didn't want him back. His mother and Jeff were doing all right without Jason. At the end of the six-month period, Jason was nearly nine and nothing had changed. In fact, Jason's behavior had deteriorated rapidly. He didn't get along with the boys in the residential treatment center; he didn't get along with anyone very well. He still lied, stole, and bullied. He still broke things and argued and hit people, and he didn't do as he was told. The consulting psychiatrist had prescribed a program of medication but discontinued the drugs after observing no appreciable changes in Jason's behavior.

Jason's case went before the Child Welfare Placement, Assessment and Review Committee (PARC) in December—the first of many reviews to come. His social worker from the Child Welfare Department was there but Jason wasn't and neither were his mother or Jeff. The conclusion of PARC, which included Jason's social worker, a psychologist, consulting psychiatrist, teachers, and supervisors, was unanimous. Although moving Jason would most likely compound his problems, Jason could no longer stay at the institution. His social worker advocated a less restrictive placement, but the response from others who knew Jason was that his problems were too severe for a regular foster home. The only alternative was to put him into a treatment foster home as soon as a bed became available. Meanwhile, he was placed in a group receiving and assessment home. His child welfare status changed to temporary guardianship.

Once a treatment foster family placement was found for Jason at the beginning of February, contacts with Jason and his family were initiated. Jason had several overnight visits with the foster family. Carol and Jeff met a few times with the treatment foster parents at their home. Meanwhile, Jason's case records from the institution and child welfare had been sent to the treatment foster care program. Meetings took place between the treatment foster care staff, the institution staff, and Jason's child welfare social worker to discuss what Jason would need from treatment foster care services. On the basis of these discussions and the treatment foster parents' observations of Jason, the treatment foster care staff decided to formulate tentative goals that were discussed with Jason before being entered into the case plan.

Within a month, Jason moved into the treatment foster care placement. His treatment foster parents, Diane and Lee Barker, had taken one other foster child since the program began and this child was still with them. When Jason arrived, there were already three children living in the home: Lee and Diane's own two children, a boy of 12 and a girl of seven, and one foster child, a boy of 10.

One of the first things Lee and Diane did was contact Jason's school to talk to his teachers about his new situation. Jason had been lucky enough to stay at the same school despite his changes in living environments so his teachers were familiar with his history. However, his behavior had been troublesome and his teachers had not related well with his mother. Much work needed to be done to establish the necessary cooperation between school and home. It was decided that Jason would have a homework book that would list the day's assignments. A school card would be stapled to the book on which the teacher would daily check off Jason's observed behaviors. How many times did he obey or fail to obey instructions? Did he hit another child? Did he make any self-praising statements or act supportively toward another student? How did he react when he was criticized or praised? Diane and Lee would look at this book every evening and focus their work with Jason on the areas that seemed to need improvement. They also kept a daily log for the other foster child in which they noted progress toward individual goals, the child's general emotional state, and any major incidents.

Jason went home to visit twice in April and his parents visited him three times in the placement. His mother had spoken to his teacher and this interview went much better than previous interviews since Jason's behavior at school had improved, his teacher felt involved in his improvement, and Jason's mother was more relaxed. There was a bake sale at school in April for which Jason's mother made cookies. There was an operetta the following month with Jason on stage and his mother and grandmother clapping in the audience. Jason made five visits home in May, three of them overnight stays, and these visits went well. Nevertheless, when the end of May came, Jeff did not want Jason to return home, and Jason's mother was uneasy about it because of Jeff's attitude.

After discussion between all the parties involved, it was decided that Jason should go home but with a lot of in-home support from the treatment foster parents and staff. A staff member would visit Jason's home as often and for as long as required, staying overnight for a week at a time if necessary. Between times, Jason's parents or Jason himself could phone the treatment parents or staff for help with any problem. The return home worked better than Jeff had expected. Jason was now doing well at school, relations between the school and his parents were good, and his mother had learned from Diane and Lee how to improve Jason's self-esteem, how to handle his aggression, and how to communicate with him. Her expectations of Jason had been reduced to expectations reasonable for a child of his age.

When Jason was 11, he transferred to the local junior high school. His reputation for being a "bad kid" still lingered and incidents were related with relish by schoolmates who remembered that Jason had hit a teacher and refused to do as he was told. Jason was approached by older boys who wanted to use his locker "to store some things." Jason agreed. He knew that the things being stored included drugs and stolen goods but by now he was one of the "in" crowd. He began to carry a knife as the others did. He experimented with drugs. He started to take an interest in the gun that Jeff had at home. Meanwhile, he was skipping classes, his grades were going down, and he was becoming increasingly aggressive toward his mother and Jeff. Jeff and his mother argued about him, Jeff saying that it had been a mistake to ever have him home, his mother pleading on his behalf, saying that it was puberty, a phase he would get over. She suggested phoning the treatment foster care staff for help but Jeff didn't want help. He didn't want a social worker present in his home. Essentially, he didn't want Jason.

One night, Jason took the gun to show to his friends at their regular meeting place. It impressed them, it raised Jason's status in the group, and he began to take it on other occasions. A few months later, the gun went off accidentally. No one was hurt but Jason was charged with careless use of firearms and received 10 days in juvenile detention with one year's probation. His parents refused to have him home when the 10 days were up, and he was sent to a group receiving and assessment placement.

After two weeks in the group receiving and assessment placement, Jason ran away and stole a motorcycle. He and his friends had engaged in a good deal of theft over the past year and Jason thought that he could manage a motorcycle without being caught. However, he was caught. He was charged with theft and spent another two days in a youth detention center where he threatened a staff member with a knife and brought on the attention of more professionals.

Despite the strong arguments of professionals who worked with Jason, his social worker believed that treatment foster care was not only the best choice for Jason, but offered the only chance for this 13-year-old to learn to live an everyday life in an everyday community. Jason's record showed that he had once been involved with treatment foster care and the treatment had seemed to be effective, at least until he entered junior high school. The treatment foster care staff made a point of asking that children who had once been with them should be referred back to them if, subsequently, they got into trouble. Accordingly, the referral was made and Jason was once more involved in the treatment foster care program.

Jason Yellowbird was now 13. He had acquired skills in theft and was familiar with alcohol, drugs, and the use of weapons; his school record and his relationship with his parents were both abysmal. He was described as sneaky and as having an oppositional disorder. Jason had become particularly aggressive when he was physically restrained for his own and others' safety. When restrained, he often lashed out at staff with obscenities. Other behaviors that made Jason difficult to care for included enuresis, nightmares, terrible hygiene and table manners, and personal property destruction, including the belongings of his peers as well as the furnishings in the room.

He was not able to live with Diane and Lee because their home was already full but another treatment foster care family was available. Since mutual support between treatment foster parents was a large component of the program and treatment parents met with each other regularly to exchange ideas about their children, Lee and Diane were able to help with the "getting acquainted" period between Jason and his new treatment foster parents. Jason met once more with Lee and Diane's own children and the foster child he had lived with before who was still with them. The people around him were therefore not entirely strange, and he was already familiar with the procedures that would be adopted.

## Jason Yellowbird's Placement Sequence

Jason first entered out-of-home care and was placed in a residential treatment center at the age of nine. He was 10 years old when he was first placed in treatment foster family care, and 13 years old at the time of his second intake to treatment foster family care. If the first residential treatment setting had been avoided and the child and family services had been directed toward the goal of surrounding this family with services in the least restrictive and most normalized environment possible, these events might have influenced Jason's subsequent behavior and adaptation back home.

**Placement History**

Home of natural parents

Residential treatment center

Group emergency home

Foster family-based treatment

Home of natural parents

Youth correctional center

Group emergency home

Ran away

Youth correctional center

Foster family-based treatment

*Goals for future living arrangements:* The aim will be for Jason to live with his natural parents, in semi-independent living, or in independent living.

*Planning for services:* Planning for Jason was undertaken on the basis of all his records to date, observations made by his treatment foster parents, and the assessment of his social worker.

## Assessment

Assessment of the family and initial attempts to assist them revealed that numerous stressors and issues affected the family, and many factors impinged on the parents' ability to take care of their child. Both parents had grown up with poor individual and family role models. Both parents had experienced rejection as well as physical and emotional abuse. Neither parent had finished high school, although both were employed and poverty was not an issue. They lived in a rented house and home management skills were often lacking. Laundry and grocery shopping were not done regularly. Marital problems persisted over the years, and both parents felt anger and hostility over their inability to manage and parent Jason. In particular, Jeff, the stepfather, felt that he was doing the best he could and did not recognize a need for improvement. Jason's mother had earlier experiences with child protection services and social workers and was not about to become involved again, particularly if her marriage was going to be sacrificed.

## Goals

General goals included increasing Jason's social competency skills, as well as drug counseling and treatment focused on increasing his positive behaviors and self-esteem. Educational competency was an important goal for him as was improved marital and family functioning for his parents. Specific treatment objectives for Jason centered around breaking his drug habit through attendance at a rehabilitation program, reducing his aggressive behaviors, reducing the number of times he stole something or lied, increasing his self-esteem and self-efficacy, improving his school grades, and improving his communication and relationship skills. Marital relationship objectives for Carole and Jeff were worked out within the context of extensive individual and couple counseling. Parenting skills have improved in many areas, but both parents tend to handle stress and new situations with a lack of self-confidence, particularly as Jason approached adulthood. They continued to have an especially difficult time in reframing negative events and feared failure in many roles. Their own childhood and adolescence has left them with huge gaps in their knowledge and sense of family life. Continued work on this area was planned. Through acceptance into the lives of the treatment foster family, who model family roles, Carol and Jeff might gain further skills in the area of parenting.

## Intervention Planning

The service model used with Jason and his family was based on the concept of "wrapping" services around the child in the family and community setting. The objectives were to facilitate behavioral, educational, and social adjustment and to prevent placement into more restrictive living environments and educational settings. In this instance, the initial goal was family reunification and the objectives were to improve the family's overall functioning as well as the manner in which Jason was parented. This was possible for some time, until his second period of out-of-home care.

As in the first placement service plan, the school was involved and Jason was given a school card and a homework book. Jason's mother and Jeff were invited to visit, but Jeff was very reluctant and it seemed less likely this time that Jason would be able to return home after a short period. Jason was involved with a probation officer and a drug rehabilitation program as well as attending school. He had difficulty remembering all his appointments, particularly since they were appointments he did not particularly want to remember. His treatment foster parents helped him to organize his time and instituted a system of small rewards for each appointment kept. The journal was brought back into play to increase communications skills and a budgeting system was introduced to help Jason manage his pocket money.

Nevertheless, all was not smooth sailing. Jason was still part of the "in" group at school, and, six months after he had moved in with his new treatment foster parents, he was involved in a motorcycle theft. His treatment foster parents and his social worker supported him through his subsequent court appearance. His social worker wrote a letter detailing his progress and he managed to avoid detention. This incident seemed to be a turning point for Jason. His treatment foster parents and the program social worker had continued to show that they cared about him, and even though he had caused more than enough trouble, he now felt that he had a family behind him. Very soon after his court appearance, he told his treatment foster parents about the "ring" at school and identified the youths involved to the school authorities. Perhaps fortunately for Jason, he was to move to senior high school in a few months' time.

Jeff was still unconvinced that Jason had reformed and resisted any suggestion that he should return home. Visits were initiated between Jason and his parents both at their home and at the treatment foster home; Jason's mother was still involved with the school, and Jason's relationship with both his parents appeared to be good. After a meeting between the foster parents, the parents, the treatment foster care staff, and Jason, it was decided that the long-term goal should be to have Jason return to his home with his mother and Jeff, and prepare him for independent living.

Jason was returned home. Over this next year, Jason will have to gradually learn to structure his own life and to accept longer term rewards as sufficient motivation for performing well in school. He now has a girlfriend and has been provided with education concerning safe sex by both sets of parents. He also has become a "big brother" to another foster boy, age nine, who was also living in the treatment foster home. Nevertheless, he still needs relatively high levels of imposed structure in order to succeed.

Separating Jason too soon from the security of his treatment foster family was considered to be inadvisable. The treatment foster care placement is, therefore, planned as a backup to a semi-independent living placement in the future so that Jason can adjust to the idea of independence at his own pace. In this way when he turns 18 he may not necessarily leave the home of his parents, but will be encouraged to move to a shared apartment within easy reach of his parents and his treatment foster parents' home. He will keep up his contact with his treatment parents so that he will have two families to support him through the stages of his independence. The treatment foster care staff continue to provide support for Jason's progress through his treatment foster parents and, to date, he and his parents are doing well.

## Evaluation

Since first entering out-of-home care Jason has experienced 10 placement changes or living environments, one runaway, and a total of five placements more restrictive than treatment foster family placement. He has lived in group emergency homes on two occasions. Jason's placement history provides a useful review of the frequency and types of out-of-home care available.

Ideally, Jason's out-of-home placements should reduce the restrictiveness of his environment and care over time. The degree of restrictiveness of each setting varied. Treatment foster family care is more restrictive than other family placements and was used here because of Jason's child welfare status, because of motivational systems implemented by the treatment parents, and because more adults were involved in the decision-making aspects of his life. Even though he still exhibits some unacceptable behavior, living in family-based settings has helped Jason develop increased socially acceptable behaviors, skills, and competencies. Decreased restrictiveness of Jason's living environment can generally be associated with movement toward the service objective of normalized living in the community. Jason's progress can also be monitored by examining the residential services time line for the level of restrictiveness of services received. Jason's service restrictiveness history indicates a reduction in placement restrictiveness and an increase in placement stability after he entered treatment foster family care.

The history of events in Jasons's life—critical behaviors, child and family life events, child and family services from birth to his sixteenth year—were used to analyze the relationships between the service delivery system and the child and family. For example, in spite of the problematic behaviors that caused Jason's initial placement in a residential setting, no services were provided to the family—except Jason's out-of-home residential child care—prior to his placement in treatment foster care and his assignment of child welfare status. Also, there is little evidence that the education services were coordinated with any other service agencies. The referral process for a more restrictive educational placement was initiated early in this child's life. The review of life events can be used to highlight the critical events and conditions in Jason's life as well as what has and has not worked and what could have been done differently. This tracking of Jason's living experiences and life events vividly shows its usefulness for clinical purposes and reveals the turbulence of his history and the damage inflicted on this child, as well as his adjustments. Serious emotional and behavioral problems began for Jason at age four and continued until he was placed in a residential setting at age nine. By the time Jason entered out-of-home care with child welfare status, he had experienced significant negative events, with a traumatic introduction into a highly restrictive setting, that most likely affected him adversely. The influence of this residential living arrangement determined important aspects of Jason's pre-placement status and the course of his adjustment while in treatment foster care each time and afterward. These frequent changes were due to his destructive, aggressive, oppositional, and noncompliant behavior, as tolerance for these behaviors diminished over time. The time line provides valuable information regarding Jason's behavioral adjustment after placement in treatment foster care on each separate occasion as well as the service delivery to him during this care. Treatment foster care providers expect children such as Jason to challenge the program, and these providers have greater than normal tolerance for such oppositional behaviors, which helped Jason stabilize. The time line indicates that treatment foster care services were coordinated and more comprehensive during this care plan than at any other time, and that there was also a decrease in Jason's problem behaviors in this period.

# CHAPTER TWELVE

# The Foxx Family: A Troubled Adolescent

The case study of the Foxx family provides opportunities for you to learn about assessing a family as well as to practice and discuss family assessment. Study questions and exercises may be done independently as a form of self-study or in peer group learning situations. Some exercises are more relevant than others to the work of particular individuals and groups. Remember that different and creative responses are acceptable as you plan interventions. The basis of this case is from my practice/research but it is essentially a composite of child and family situations.

## Questions

1. As the biological parent, foster parent, social worker, parent aide, judge, or agency administrator in this case, what do you see as your primary obligation?

2. What are the main goals you see in this case, particularly in relation to family reunification? Who is the family?

3. What is the biggest challenge this case presents in terms of family reunification? What family subsystems need to be changed and what changes are necessary?

4. What would you need from the other community service providers to reach case goals?

5. What are, or could be, obstacles to meeting case goals?

# Case Study: John Foxx

## Identifying Information

*Parents:*

Jennifer Smith, age 35, now living in Colorado

Samuel Foxx, age 38, now living in Niagara Falls

*Children:*

John, age 16

*Race:* Native American

*Religion:* Roman Catholic

*Languages:*

*Parents' occupation:*

*Referral source:* Child Protective Services (CPS)

## Presenting Problem

John Foxx, now age 16, was born when Jennifer Smith was 19 years old and when Samuel Foxx was 22. His mother recalls both her pregnancy and the delivery of John as difficult. She feels that there were likely some complications at the time of birth. Jennifer describes her relationship with Samuel as physically abusive. She was battered both during and after her pregnancy. When John was approximately seven months of age, she left Samuel and moved to Denver, Colorado, where she presently resides. Samuel did not remain involved in John's life, although he made sure that John was registered with the Blood Tribe on Samuel's reservation at birth.

John's first contact with Child Protective Services was at the age of three, when he was found wandering in his neighborhood. He had apparently unlocked his baby-sitter's door and left while his mother was working. After the second occasion that he was found wandering, his mother was given information on choosing appropriate child care and referred for observation in a special child care center for toddlers and to her family medical doctor.

At the age of six, in grade one, John was the subject of a police report sent to Child Protective Services (CPS) for information only, regarding John's theft of a bicycle. The police had caught John, returned the bicycle, and at the request of his mother, spoken to John sternly about the theft. Approximately one week after the police report was sent in October, John's school principal contacted Child Protective Services (CPS) reporting that John was threatening other children on the school grounds with a knife. When the concerns were investigated, Jennifer indicated that while John had always been a challenge to manage, his behavior had worsened approximately four months earlier, in June, when he had been severely battered by the spouse of his baby-sitter. A police complaint had been made after the incident and a warrant issued for the arrest of the abuser, who had already left the state. Jennifer had concerns about possible neurological damage to John as a result of the beating. Jennifer was described as appropriate in her parenting and in developing more effective strategies for managing her son's behavior. The file was closed in December, three months after the report was initially taken.

The school again contacted CPS in February, two months after the closure of the file. Jennifer was contacted but no services were offered. Five months after the file was reopened, CPS was contacted by Jennifer and her therapist, requesting services due to physical and emotional abuse of Jennifer and John, by Jennifer's common-law spouse. Jennifer and the school had moved John to a specialized school program for children with severe management problems. The abuse was disclosed to the therapist working with the family. John was seven years old at this time.

Two months following the disclosure of the physical abuse, a supervision order was requested in family court. A two-month adjournment was granted in order to serve court documents to the common-law spouse. On the return to court, a four-month supervision order was granted. At the end of the supervision order, in April, Jennifer then agreed to a voluntary support agreement and the order was allowed to lapse. The school contacted Child Protective Services again in June, shortly after John's eighth birthday, indicating that John was exposing himself to other children at school. During this period of time, Jennifer gave birth to a healthy baby boy.

The family was reportedly doing well when they moved in September with the common-law partner to his reservation. Jennifer was working full time at a seasonal position and was commuting to the reservation on weekends. Her common-law husband was looking after the children. The file was transferred to the social services department on the reservation and was closed in February.

In the same month the file was closed, Jennifer left her partner and returned to the city. Jennifer contacted Child Protective Services with concerns about John and requesting a residential program. John's behaviors included stealing, lying, hurting small animals, running away from home, and managing his anger poorly. Also, according to the file, John was either not wiping himself well after bowel movements or was soiling his pants.

Child Protective Services was able to place John in a receiving and assessment home immediately and to reconnect Jennifer and John with the therapist who had been involved when John was seven. In March, a school report assessed John as inadequate academically, using avoidance techniques (such as talk avoidance), afraid of making mistakes, having difficulty with peers, and behaving aggressively.

A neurological assessment was requested and scheduled based on Jennifer's information about John's battering by his former baby-sitter's spouse. There was no evidence of follow through. Questions were also raised regarding a possible Attention Deficit Hyperactive Disorder. The pediatrician involved did not recommend an assessment.

By July, at age nine, John was returned home to the care of his mother and her common-law partner, who had reconciled with Jennifer. Jennifer had completed an intensive parenting program and her partner had been referred to a program for men who batter. Jennifer was again employed seasonally and the partner was looking after the children.

In August, John was again placed in a foster home and concerns were raised regarding his treatment of animals. John was returned home and in September an emergency placement was located in a treatment facility.

Two years later, in October, John was apprehended and a temporary care order was granted. Three months later, in January, a termination of parental rights order was granted. Since John has come into the foster care system he has experienced approximately 51 placements. The high number may be partly because of John's tendency to run away and partly because of the inability of foster parents to manage his behavior. The majority of John's placements were in group care. John has been in and out of juvenile offenders' facilities since the age of 13. He was sexually abused at the age of 12 while in care, and is believed to be a sexual offender himself, although there is nothing written to support this belief.

John continues to have contact with his mother and his three half-siblings. She is not included in the planning for John because she no longer has parental rights. John initiates the majority of the contacts. John's biological father was located when John was 12, as John had requested contact with his father. Nothing resulted from this contact.

John is presently 17 years of age, has approximately a grade seven education, has no job or life skills, and continues to present the same behaviors that brought him into care. John is described as angry and aggressive. He lies and steals. His primary coping strategies are abusing drugs and alcohol, running away, and sleeping. He is likely depressed but unlikely to take medication on a regular basis. Although he is of native American descent, on his father's side, he does not identify with his father's tribe. He is presently in a juvenile offenders' center for auto theft. It is possible that his sentence will extend at least to his eighteenth birthday, at which time his child welfare status will end.

## Assessment Plan for John Foxx

It would appear likely that John has some neurological damage. This could be from difficulties experienced during his mother's pregnancy and delivery, from the severe battering he received from a baby-sitter's spouse when he was six, and/or from factors unknown.

John experienced severe abuse from his mother's common-law partner. When John was 12, a peer reportedly sexually assaulted him while they were in a treatment facility. It is possible that John has experienced other abuse that we are not aware of.

The result is that John has difficulty problem solving, needs constant repetition to learn new information, and must have short-term concrete goals to learn new behavior. John appears to function most effectively in a highly structured environment; however, he resists structure when he is not in a restrictive setting. John has typically not done well in group living situations, such as group homes. John's strengths include his desire to visit with his father and to learn to live independently. He has volunteered to work in the kitchen twice per day while in the Colorado Youth Offenders' Center, to learn new skills and become productive. John is able to identify his deficits and areas for growth. He has also shown a desire to remain connected to his family and has taken responsibility for maintaining his relationship with his mother.

Several recommendations that might positively influence John's future are presently being pursued for him.

1. John needs to be allowed the opportunity to develop the skills necessary to experience some success as an independent adult. This would include actively pursuing a supported independent living situation, as John has requested. John should also be helped to find an educational placement that would address his specific learning needs. The Family Networks Program believes that John's child welfare status should be extended, with John's consent, in order to allow for these conditions to be realized.

2. John needs an opportunity to visit with his family in Michigan with supervision and support for both John and his family.

3. John should be provided with the opportunity and support to explore his culture and heritage, including traditional spiritual healing. A Native mentor has consented to see John while he is incarcerated to allow him to explore traditional Native spirituality. John would benefit from exposure to traditional activities while visiting with his family in Michigan

John has difficulty developing and maintaining relationships and appears to use distancing tactics, such as running away, to avoid allowing others to become close to him. John anticipates that he will let people down and he may deliberately sabotage relationships that are important to him. Like most children with John's history, he has learned survival skills, including not letting others know your weaknesses and not trusting others quickly. John has shut down his feelings for such an extended period of time that he appears to have limited ability to express or identify his feelings. This may be why his predominant emotion, particularly under stress, is displayed as anger. John's primary coping strategies are running away, using drugs and alcohol, reacting with anger, and sleeping. John shows symptoms of depression including his sleeping pattern, his slow movement, and general history, which would all be risk factors for depression. John's history notwithstanding, he typically presents to people as a young man who has great potential that has been given little opportunity to flourish. He can demonstrate caring for others.

# References

Alexander, J. F., & Parsons, B. V. (1982). *Functional family therapy.* Pacific Grove, CA: Brooks/Cole.

Alexander, L. B., & Luborsky, L. (1986). The Penn Helping Alliance Scales. In L. S. Greenberg & W. M. Pinsof (Eds.), *The psychotherapeutic process: A research handbook* (pp. 325–366). New York: The Guilford Press.

Allender, J., Carey, K., Garcia-Castanon, J., Garcia, B., Gonzalez, B., Hedge, G., Herrell, A., Kiyuna, R., Rector, C., & Henderson-Sparks, J. (1997). Interprofessional collaboration training project. California State University, Fresno. (Available from Teaching Research Division, Western Oregon State College, Monmouth, Oregon 97361)

American Psychiatric Association. (1994). *Diagnostic and statistical manual of mental disorders* (4th ed.). Washington, DC: Author.

Ammerman, R. T., & Hersen, M. (Eds.) (1999). *Assessment of family violence: A clinical and legal sourcebook.* (2nd ed.). New York: John Wiley.

Bandura, A. (1977). *Social learning theory.* Englewood Cliffs, NJ: Prentice-Hall.

Bavolek, S. J. (1984). *Handbook for the Adult-Adolescent Parenting Inventory.* Eau Claire, WI: Family Development Associates.

Beavers, W. R., & Hampson, R. (1990). *Successful families: Assessment and intervention.* New York: Norton.

Beier, E. G., & Sternberg, D. P. (1977). Marital communication. *Journal of Communication, 27,* 92–100.

Bronfenbrenner, U. (1986). Ecology of the family as a context for human development research perspectives. *Developmental Psychology, 22,* 723–742.

Buri, J. R., Misukanis, T. M., & Mueller, R. A. (1994). Parental Nurturance Scale. In *Measures for clinical practice: A sourcebook* (Vol. 1, 2nd ed., pp. 388–389). New York: Free Press.

Burns, G. L., & Patterson, D. R. (1990). Conduct problem behaviors in a stratified random sample of children and adolescents: New standardization data on the Eyberg Child Behavior Inventory. *Psychological Assessment, 2,* 391–397.

Campis, L. K., Lyman, R. D., & Prentice-Dunn, S. (1986). The Parental Locus of Control Scale: Development and validation. *Journal of Clinical Child Psychiatry, 15,* 260–267.

Carter, B., & McGoldrick, M. (1998). Overview: The changing family life cycle: A framework for family therapy. In B. Carter & M. McGoldrick (Eds.), *The changing family life cycle: A framework for family therapy* (2nd ed.) Boston: Allyn & Bacon.

Cicchetti, D., & Lynch, M. (1993). Toward an ecological/transactional model of community violence and child maltreatment: Consequences for children's development. Children and violence [Special issues]. *Psychiatry: Interpersonal and Biological Process, 56,* 96–118.

Colapinto, J. (1982). Structural family therapy. In A. Horn & M. Ohlsen (Eds.), *Family counseling and therapy* (pp.112–140). Itasca, IL: F. E. Peacock.

Corcoran, J. (2000). *Evidence-based social work practice with families. A lifespan approach.* New York: Springer Series on Social Work.

Corcoran, K. (1992). *Structuring change: Effective practice for common client problems.* Chicago: Lyceum Books.

Corcoran, K., & Fischer, J. (1994). *Measures for clinical practice* (2nd ed., Vols. 1–2). New York: Free Press.

Corcoran, K., & Gingerich, W. (1992). Practice evaluation: Setting goals, measuring change. In *Structuring change: Effective practice for common client problems* (pp. 255–271). Chicago: Lyceum Books.

Corcoran, K., & Videka-Sherman, L. (1992). Some things we know about effective clinical social work. In K. Corcoran (Ed.), *Structuring change: Effective practice for common client problems* (pp. 15–27). Chicago: Lyceum Books.

Cross, T., Bazron, B., Dennis, K., & Issacs, M. (1989). *Towards a culturally competent system of care: A monograph on effective services for minority children who are severely emotionally disturbed.* Washington, DC: Georgetown University Child Development Center, National Technical Assistance Center for Children's Mental Health.

DiMaria, R., Weeks, G., & Hof, L. (1999). *Focused genograms: Intergenerational assessment of individuals, couples, and families.* Philadelphia, PA: Brunner/Mazel.

Eggeman, K., Moxley, V., & Schumm, W. R. (1985). Assessing spouses' perceptions of Gottman's Temporal Form in marital conflict. *Psychological Reports, 57,* 171–181.

Elkind, D. (1994). *Ties that stress: The new family imbalance.* Cambridge, MA: Harvard University Press.

Epstein, N., Baldwin, L., & Bishop, D. (1983). The McMaster Family Assessment Device. *Journal of Marital and Family Therapy, 9,* 171–180.

Epstein, N., & Bishop, D. (1981). Problem-centered systems therapy of the family. In A. Gurman & D. Kniskern (Eds.), *Handbook of family therapy* (pp. 444–482). New York: Brunner/Mazel.

Fantuzzo, J., McDermott, P., & Lutz, M. N. (1999). Clinical issues in the assessment of family violence involving children. In R. T. Ammerman & M. Hersen (Eds.), *Assessment of family violence: A clinical and legal sourcebook* (2nd ed), pp.10–23. New York: John Wiley.

Fine, M. A., & Schwebel, A. I. (1983). Long-term effects of divorce on parent-child relationships. *Developmental Psychology, 19,* 703–713.

Fischer, J., & Corcoran, K. (1994). *Measures for clinical practice: A sourcebook.* (2nd ed., Vol. I). New York: Free Press.

Fleuridas, C., Nelson, T. S., & Rosenthal, D. M. (1986). The evolution of circular questions: Training family therapists. *Journal of Marital and Family Therapy, 12,* 120–125.

Franklin, C., & Jordan, C. (Eds.). (1999). *Family practice: Brief systems methods for social work.* Pacific Grove, CA: Brooks/Cole.

Franklin, C., & Jordan, C. (1992). Teaching students to perform assessments. *Journal of Social Work Education. 28*(2), 222–241.

Fraser, M. (Ed.). (1997). *Risk and resilience in childhood: An ecological perspective.* Washington, DC: NASW Press.

Gambrill, E. (1997). *Social work practice: A critical thinker's guide.* New York: Oxford University Press.

Garner, J. W., & Hudson, W. W. (1992). Non-Physical Abuse of Partner Scale and the Physical Abuse of Partner Scale. In W. W. Hudson, (Ed.) *The WALMYR Assessment Scales Scoring Manual.* Tempe, AZ: WALMYR Publishing.

Gibbs, L., & Gambrill, E. (1999). *Critical thinking for social workers* (rev. ed.). Thousand Oaks, CA: Pine Forge Press.

Goldenberg, I., & Goldenberg, H. (2000). *Family therapy: An overview* (5th ed.). Pacific Grove, CA: Wadsworth.

Goldner, V., Penn, P., Sheinberg, M., & Walker, G. (1990). Love and violence: Gender paradoxes in volatile attachments. *Family Process, 29,* 348–364.

Green, R. J., & Werner, P. D. (1996). Intrusiveness and closeness caregiving: Rethinking the concept of family enmeshment. *Family Process, 35,* 115–136.

Gurman, A. S., & Kniskern, D. (Eds.). (1981). *Handbook of family therapy.* New York: Brunner/Mazel.

Henggeler, S. W., Schoenwald, S. K., Bordin, C. M., Rowland, M. D., & Cunningham, P. B. (1998). *Multisystemic treatment of antisocial behavior in children and adolescents.* New York: Guilford Press.

Hepworth, D. H., Rooney, R., & Larsen, J. A. (1997). *Direct social work practice: Theory and skills* (5th ed.). Pacific Grove, CA: Brooks/Cole.

Horowitz, M. J., Wilner, N., & Alvarez, W. (1979). Impact of event scale: A measure of subjective stress. *Psychosomatic Medicine, 41,* 209–218.

Hudson, W. W. (1982). *The clinical measurement package.* Pacific Grove, CA: Brooks/Cole

Hudson, W. W. (1990a). *The WALMYR Assessment Scales Scoring Manual.* Tempe, AZ: WALMYR Publishing.

Hudson, W. W. (1990b). *The MPSI Manual.* Tempe, AZ: WALMYR Publishing.

Hudson, W. W. (1992a). *MPSI Technical Manual.* Tempe, AZ: WALMYR Publishing.

Hudson, W. W. (1992b). *The WALMYR Assessment Scales Scoring Manual.* Tempe, AZ: WALMYR Publishing.

Hudson, W. W., & Garner, J. W. (1992). Index of Alcohol Involvement. In W. W. Hudson (Ed.), *The WALMYR Assessment Scales Scoring Manual.* Tempe, AZ: WALMYR Publishing.

Huffman, L., Mehlinger, S., & Kerivan, A. (2000). *Off to a Good Start.* Chapel Hill: University of North Carolina, FPG Child Development Center.

Hughes, R. (1999, May). The meaning of "evidence based" services in PSR. *International Association of Psychosocial Rehabilitation Services (IAPSRS), 2,* 1–10.

Illinois Department of Social Services. (1985). *Child abuse and neglect investigations decisions handbook.* Springfield, IL: Author.

Imber Coppersmith, E. (1983). The place of family therapy in the homeostasis of larger systems. In M. Aronson & R. Wolberg (Eds.), *Group and family therapy: An overview* (pp. 216–227). New York: Brunner/Mazel.

Ivanoff, A., & Stern, S. B. (1992). Self-management interventions in health and mental health settings: Evidence of maintenance and generalization. *Social Work Research & Abstracts, 28*(4), 32–38.

Jordan, C., & Franklin, C. (1995). *Clinical assessment for social workers: Quantitative and qualitative methods.* Chicago: Lyceum Press.

Kilpatrick, A. C., & Holland, T. P. (1995). *Working with families: An integrative model by level of functioning.* Needham Heights, MA: Allyn & Bacon.

Magura, S., & Moses, B. (1986). *Rating form for Child Well-Being Scales.* Washington, DC: Child Welfare League of America.

Magura, S., Moses, B. S., & Jones, M. A. (1987). *Assessing risk and measuring change of families: The family risk scales.* Washington, DC: Child Welfare League of America.

Marks, J., & McDonald, T. (1989). *Risk assessment in child protective services: 4. Predicting recurrence of child maltreatment.* Portland: University of Southern Maine.

Mattaini, M. (1999). *Clinical interventions with families.* Washington, DC: NASW Press.

McCubbin, H. I., Boss, P. G., Wilson, L. R., & Dahl, B. B. (1991). Family Coping Inventory. In H. I. McCubbin and A. I. Thompson (Eds.), *Family assessment inventories for research and practice.* Madison: University of Wisconsin Press.

McCubbin, H. I., Patterson, J. M., Bauman, E., & Harris, L. H. (1991). Adolescent-Family Inventory of Life Events and Changes. In H. I. McCubbin & A. I. Thompson (Eds.), *Family assessment inventories for research and practice.* Madison: University of Wisconsin Press.

McCubbin, M. A., McCubbin, H. I., & Thompson, A. I. (1991). Family Hardiness Index. In H. I. McCubbin and A. I. Thompson (Eds.), *Family assessment inventories for research and practice.* Madison: University of Wisconsin Press.

McGill, D. (1992, June). The cultural story in multicultural family therapy. *Families in Society: The Journal of Contemporary Human Services, 73,* 339–349.

Minuchin, S. (1974). *Families and family therapy.* Cambridge, MA: Harvard University Press.

Mulvey, E., Arthur, M., & Reppucci, D. (2000). The prevention of juvenile delinquency: A review of the research. *The prevention researcher online.* http://tpronline.org/articles/

Nichols, M. P., & Schwartz, R. C. (1995). *Family therapy: Concepts and methods.* (3rd ed.). Needham Heights, MA: Allyn & Bacon.

Nichols, M. P., & Schwartz, R. C. (1998). *Family therapy: Concepts and methods.* (4th ed.). Needham Heights, MA: Allyn & Bacon.

Okun, B. (1996). *Understanding diverse families: What practitioners need to know.* New York: Guilford Press.

Parker, G., Tupling, H., & Brown, L. B. (1979). A Parental Bonding Instrument. *British Journal of Medical Psychology, 52,* 1–10.

Paul, R. W., & Binker, A. J. (Eds.). (1990). *Critical thinking: What every person needs to survive in a rapidly changing world.*

Rohnert Park, CA: Center for Critical Thinking and Moral Critique, Sonoma State University.

Reamer, F. G. (1995). Ethics and values. *Encyclopedia of Social Work* (19th ed., pp. 893–902). Washington, DC: NASW Press.

Reimer, M., Thomlison, B., & Bradshaw, C. (1999). *The clinical rotation handbook.* Albany, NY: Delmar.

Rothery, M. (1999). The resources of intervention. In F. J. Turner (Ed.), *Social work practice: A Canadian perspective* (pp. 34–47). Scarborough, Ontario: Prentice-Hall.

Rothery, M., & Enns, G. (in press). Haworth Press.

Sargent, G. A. (1985). *The use of rituals in family therapy: When, where, and why.* Paper presented at the AFTA Conference in San Diego, CA.

Sattler, J. (1998). *Clinical and forensic interviewing of children and families: Guidelines for the mental health, education, pediatric, and child maltreatment fields.* San Diego, CA: Jerome M. Sattler.

Stiffman, A. R., Orme, J. G., Evans, D. A., Feldman, R. A., & Keeney, P. A. (1984). A brief measure of children's behavior problems: The Behavior Rating Index for Children. *Measurement and Evaluation in Counseling and Development, 16,* 83–90.

Straus, M. A., & Gelles, R. J. (1990). *Physical violence in American families: Risk factors and adaptations to violence in 8,145 families.* New Brunswick, NJ: Transaction.

Thomlison, B., & Bradshaw, C. (1999). The accountable clinical social worker: Evaluating change. In F. J. Turner (Ed.), *Social work practice: A Canadian perspective* (pp. 164–178). Scarborough, Ontario, Canada: Prentice Hall/Allyn & Bacon.

Thomlison, B., & Bradshaw, C. (in press). Clinical practice evaluation. In F. J. Turner (Ed.), *Social work practice: A Canadian perspective* (2nd ed.). Scarborough, Ontario, Canada: Prentice Hall/Allyn & Bacon.

Thomlison, B., & Thomlison, R. (1996). Behavior theory and social work treatment. In F. J. Turner (Ed.), *Social work treatment: Interlocking theoretical perspectives* (4th ed., pp. 39–68). New York: Free Press.

Thomlison, R. J. (1984). Something works: Evidence from practice effectiveness studies. *Social Work, 19,* 51–57.

Thornton, T., Craft, C., Dahlberg, L., Lynch, B., & Baer, K. (2000). *Best practices of youth violence prevention: A sourcebook for community action.* Atlanta: Centers for Disease Control and Prevention, National Center for Injury Prevention and Control.

Thyer, B. A. (Ed.). (1989). *Behavioral family therapy.* Springfield: Charles C. Thomas.

Thyer, B. A. (1994). Social work theory and practice research: The approach of logical positivism. *Social Work and Social Services Review, 4,* 5–26.

Thyer, B. A., & Wodarski, J. S. (Eds.). (1998). *Handbook of empirical social work practice* (Vol. 1). New York: John Wiley.

Tomm, K. (1984). One perspective on the Milan systemic approach: 2. Description of session format, interviewing style, and interventions. *Journal of Marital and Family Therapy, 10*(3), 252–271.

Tomm, K., & Sanders, G. (1983). Family assessment in a problem-oriented record. In J. C. Hansen & B. F. Keeny (Eds.), *Diagnosis and assessment in family therapy* (pp.101–122). London: Aspen Systems Corporation.

Tripodi, T. (1994). *A primer on single-subject design for clinical social workers.* Washington, DC: NASW.

Tutty, L. (1990). The response of community mental health professionals to clients' rights: A review and suggestions. *Canadian Journal of Community Mental Health, 9,* 1–24.

Tutty, L. (1995). Theoretical and practical issues in selecting a measure of family functioning. *Research on Social Work Practice, 5*(1), 80–106.

Wald, M., & Woolverton, N. (1990). Risk assessment. *Child Welfare, 69,* 483–511.

Weiss, C. H. (1995). Nothing as practical as good theory: Exploring theory-based evaluation for comprehensive community initiatives for children and families. In J. P. Connell, A. C. Kubisch, L. B. Schorr, & C. H. Weiss (Eds.), *New approaches to evaluating community initiatives: Concepts, methods, and contexts.* Washington, DC: Aspen Institute.

Whittaker, J., Schinke, S., & Gilchrist, L. (1986). The ecological paradigm in child, youth, and family services: Implications for policy and practice. *Social Service Review, 60,* 483–503.

Williams, J. & Ell, K. (1998). *Advances in mental health research: Implications for practice.* Washington, DC: NASW Press.

Wright, L., & Leahey, M. (1984). *Nurses and families: A guide to family assessment and intervention* . Philadelphia, PA: F. A. Davis.

Wright, L., & Leahey, M. (1994). *Nurses and families: A guide to family assessment and intervention* (2nd ed.). Philadelphia, PA: F. A. Davis.

Wright, L., Watson, W., & Bell, J. (1996). *Beliefs: The heart of healing in families and illness.* New York: Basic Books, Harper-Collins.

Zastrow, C. (1995). *The practice of social work* (5th ed.). Pacific Grove, CA: Brooks/Cole.

Zinn, M., & Eitzen, D. (1990). *Diversity in families* (2nd ed.). New York: Harper-Collins.

# *Index*

checklists
    ethical concerns, 14
    family strengths, 77–78
child maltreatment measures, 92–93
child problem measures, 91
Child Well-Being Scales, 93
Child's Attitude Toward Father and Mother Scales, 91
circular causality, 38–40
circular questions, examples of, 39
*Clinical Assessment for Social Workers,* 25
*Clinical Measurement Package,* 25
cognitive thinking, changing, 78–79
confidentiality, 11–12
    *See also* ethical issues
Conflict Tactics Scales, 92
context for family practice, 32–33
contract with the family, stating goals, 76–77
cooperation skills, scale for, 70
critical thinking skills
    assessment and intervention process and, 18–19
    meaning of, 102
    practitioner's beliefs and values, 6
    and self-assessment, 103
cultural information, questions about, 43
culturally sensitive assessments, 71
culture and families, 41–43

## D

death of wife and mother, case study, 137–146
Del Sol family case, 125–135
developmental-ecological perspective, and assessment, 24
*Diagnostic and Statistical Manual for Mental Disorders (DSM-IV),* 24
diary writing, compared to journal writing, 102
disengagement, and boundary problems, 37

## E

ecomaps
    blank ecomap, 63
    for boundary illustration, 36
    child's ecomap, 65
    for connected systems, 35
    constructing, 62–63
    for cultural information, 43
    sample family ecomap, 64
emotional connections, of families, 32
enmeshment, and boundary problems, 37
ethical decision-making protocol, 9–11
ethical issues
    checklist of ethical concerns, 14
    maintaining ethical standards, 9–12
    practitioner and, 5–6
evaluation tools. *See* measurement and evaluation tools

## F

FAD. *See* Family Assessment Device
families and environments, multisystem perspective, 18
family
    culture and, 41–43
    defined, 4–5
    development of, 40–41
    imbalances in structure of, 30–31
    new types of, 30, 41
    rituals and traditions of, 44–45
family and environmental stress measures, 93–94
Family Assessment Device (FAD), 89, 90
family assessment report. *See* assessment report
family beliefs and values, 7–8, 43–44
    assessments and interventions and, 29–30
family-centered approach, 33
Family Coping Inventory, 94
family development
    attachments, 41
    states of, 40
    tasks, 40–41
family engagement, 19–20
family functioning, 45–48
    measures of, 90–91
Family Hardiness Index, 94
family information, guidelines for gathering, 17
Family Risk Scales, 93
family scales, 26
family strengths, 77–78
family systems approach
    key assumptions, 31–33
    key concepts, 33–40
    overview, 3–4
    theoretical basis for assessment, 31–40
family tree. *See* genograms
family violence measures, 92
first-order change, 76
Foxx family case, 159–163

## G

General Functioning Scale, 90
genograms, 57–62
    blank genogram, 59
    for boundary illustration, 36
    constructing, 58–63
    for cultural information, 43
    guidelines, 61–62
    sample family genogram, 61
    symbols for, 60
graphic tools. *See* mapping and graphic tools
grids. *See* social network map and grid
guidelines
    ethical decision-making protocol, 9–10
    for gathering family information, 17

## I

Illinois CANTS, 93
Impact of Events Scale, 93
Index of Alcohol Involvement, 93
Index of Family Relations (IFR), 89, 91
Index of Marital Satisfaction, 92
individualized measures, 88
    *See also* mapping and graphic tools; self-report
        tools
interventions, 75–86
    boundary changes, 83–84
    described, 75
    family strengths, 77–80
    goals for, 76–77
    opportunities for support, 80–81
    parent and family-based strategies, 82–83
    planning for, 75–76
    selecting, 81–82
    solution identification, 77
interviewing the family, 53–57
    first interview guidelines, 55–57
    preparing for, 54–55
    questions for first interview, 58
    stages of, 56–57
    techniques for, 25–26

## J

joining with the family system, 52
journal writing
    life summary profile, 105–109
    purpose of, 103–104
    for self-assessment, 102–103
    starting, 103

## K

Kansas Marital Conflict Scale, 92

## L

legal requirements, 9
    confidentiality, 11–12
levels of family functioning, 47
life summary profile, 105–109
linear causality, 38

## M

mandated reporting, confidentiality and, 11–12
mapping and graphic tools, 26
    for assessment, 57–66
    *See also* ecomaps; genograms; social network
        map and grid

marital conflict
    case study about, 125–135
    measures of, 92
McCoy family case, 137–146
measurement and evaluation tools, 87–97
    for common family problems, 90–94
    evaluating change, 94–96
    guidelines for using, 89–90
    selecting, 87–89
Multi-Problem Screening Inventory (MPSI), 90, 91,
    92, 93
multisystem perspective, on families and environ-
    ments, 18

## N

National Association of Social Workers (NASW),
    code of ethics, 11
Non-Physical Abuse of Partner Scale, 92

## O

observational techniques, 26
open-ended interviews, 25–26

## P

parent and family-based intervention strategies,
    82–83
Parent-Child Relationship Survey, 91
Parental Bonding Instrument, 92
Parental Locus of Control Scale, 92
Parental Nurturance Scale, 92
parenting skills
    case study about, 125–135
    measures of, 91–92
Partner Abuse Scale, 92
personal beliefs
    assessments and interventions and, 29–30
    practitioner and, 6–7
Physical Abuse of Partner Scale, 92
practice setting beliefs, 8
practitioner's beliefs and values, 8
    examining your family experience, 101–111
    *See also* personal beliefs
professional beliefs and values, 5–6, 8
purpose of assessment, 22–24

## Q

qualitative assessments, 25
quantitative assessments, 25